Praise for Jessica F

Love. Wisdom. Mother

'A cathartic read for any new mother struggling with the pain of adjustment.' *Herald Sun*

'Distinctive for its honesty . . . This is a book that new or expectant mothers will find great comfort in and much practical common sense.' *Weekly Times*

'A loving, honest tome . . . Rowe has provided us with an exquisite collection of varied motherhood experiences.' Sophia Whitfield

Is This My Beautiful Life?

'Rowe's unglossy account resonates far beyond the glare of the studio lights. Her honesty shatters the mask of stoicism worn by many successful women . . . the impact of her revealing memoir should not be underestimated. Amid the turmoil, there is beauty in Rowe's imperfect life and it is more than skin deep.' *Sydney Morning Herald*

'Offering encouragement, sympathy and comfort to women who may find themselves struggling with "having it all", *Is This My Beautiful Life?* is an open and touching read, addressing an important subject that affects around 1 in 7 Australian women.' *Book'd Out*

'Jessica writes with refreshing honesty about her journey through motherhood so far.' *Mamamia*

'Jessica has parlayed her tendency to "over-share" into an honest dialogue that intends to abolish stigmas and encourage greater support.' *Australian Traveller*

'A touching memoir by a woman trying to make a difference when it comes to openness about mental health issues.' *Law Society Journal NSW*

Jessica Rowe is an accomplished journalist, television presenter, speaker and author.

Jessica has written three bestselling non-fiction books: *The Best of Times, the Worst of Times* (co-authored with Penelope Rowe); *Love. Wisdom. Motherhood.*; and her memoir, *Is This My Beautiful Life?*

A proud 'crap housewife' herself, Jessica has gathered a strong and loyal following on her #craphousewife website, Facebook and Instagram. She celebrates and unites all mothers who sometimes feel they are not perfect.

Jessica also co-creates a hilarious and wise podcast with best friend and television icon Denise Drysdale, called *One Fat Lady and One Thin Lady.*

A passionate advocate for mental health awareness, Jessica is an ambassador for beyondblue and a patron of Mental Health Australia. In 2015, she was awarded a Member of the Order of Australia for both her advocacy work and contribution to Australian media.

Jessica is married to journalist Peter Overton and they have two young daughters.

For more information, please go to jessicarowe.com.au, craphousewife.com and watercooler.net.au. And you can follow Jessica's Instagram adventures on @jessjrowe.

JESSICA ROWE

Diary of a
CRAP
HOUSEWIFE

ALLEN&UNWIN
SYDNEY·MELBOURNE·AUCKLAND·LONDON

Allen & Unwin
83 Alexander Street
Crows Nest NSW 2065
Australia
Phone: (61 2) 8425 0100
Email: info@allenandunwin.com
Web: www.allenandunwin.com

 A catalogue record for this book is available from the National Library of Australia

ISBN 978 1 76052 952 9

The recipe for Tuna Niçoise Salad on page 81 is a modified version of a recipe originally published in *Dinner with Justine* by Justine Schofield (Pan Macmillan, 2016), reproduced with permission from the publisher.

The recipe for Chicken and Pesto Spaghetti on page 216 is a modified version of a recipe originally published in *Simple Every Day* by Justine Schofield (Pan Macmillan, 2017), reproduced with permission from the publisher.

Set in 12/19.2 pt Didot LH by Bookhouse, Sydney
Printed and bound in Australia by Griffin Press

10 9 8 7 6 5 4 3 2

MIX
Paper from
responsible sources
FSC® C009448

The paper in this book is FSC® certified. FSC® promotes environmentally responsible, socially beneficial and economically viable management of the world's forests.

For Allegra and Giselle,
you are my greatest joy

Be silly. Be honest. Be kind.

RALPH WALDO EMERSON

Contents

Introduction

Housework can't kill you, but why take a chance?

PHYLLIS DILLER

I'm a proud crap housewife! What does that mean? It's my way of being lighthearted so I can take the pressure off myself and realise that I *am* good enough. I'm also an over-sharer, far from perfect and I get through some days better than others with the help of my family, friends, cats, chocolate and antidepressants. I had postnatal depression after the birth of both of my daughters and struggled to ask for help because of the pressure I'd put on myself to be a 'perfect mother'. Of course, I now realise there is no such thing as being a perfect mother, wife, friend and career woman! Besides, how boring life would be if you had it all together, all the time.

How did I see the imperfect light? It took time and I've wasted too much energy keeping up appearances over the years. Sometimes I still slip up and I'm not sure any of us every really stop trying to get it right. But for me, that is the joy of living—always learning about myself and about who and what matters. The older I get, the more comfortable I am with letting people and situations go because they don't matter. How much time have you wasted worrying about what other people think? Especially those you don't really like or respect?

I now wear my so-called 'failings' and 'flaws' like badges of honour as I've discovered the enormous power that comes from being vulnerable. Part of that vulnerability has meant letting go of the apron strings tied around the airbrushed image of what a family is 'supposed' to look like.

Sometimes this means I feed my tribe toast for dinner. It also means having dirty dishes in the sink unless my husband is around because he finds it therapeutic to wash them. We have cupboards that are hastily jammed with stuff when unexpected visitors arrive, as well as those never-ending piles of clothes in laundry baskets dotted around our house. Our family doesn't own an iron. If you give your clothes a quick, forceful shake and put them on straight out of the dryer, all the creases disappear. I discovered only recently that my smallest daughter didn't know what an iron was when we were playing charades together. I was over-acting (as per usual) and miming putting up an ironing board and pressing a shirt.

'Are you stretching?' asked Giselle.

'No,' I replied.

'You're not meant to talk, Mummy! Do you have a sore wrist?'

Shaking my head, I tried again and again to imitate the motion of ironing. Eventually I had to pause our game and google images of irons to show my daughter what I was trying to do.

#CRAPHOUSEWIFE

Craphousewife.com began like so many other parts of my life—through a conversation. I'm someone who has always loved a chat! Before talking at a writers' festival in Brisbane, I bonded over caffeine with the woman who was going to interview me on stage. Her name was Lauren Sams, also an author and a journalist, and we both had young kids of a similar age. The pair of us were having a mutual moan about the juggle of trying to be a 'good' mum. Lauren told me about an Instagram account about school lunches where parents posted pictures of the intricate and fancy-looking lunches they made for their children each day. Think pirate-shaped sandwiches, homemade nut-free muesli bars and star-shaped fruit speared onto blunted vegan wooden skewers. Surely this was a joke?

But it wasn't—when I logged onto the account I was horrified at this perfection being paraded in front of me. Initially, I reacted with that all-too-familiar feeling of not being up to scratch; my daughters got a Vegemite sandwich in their lunch orders most days. Their morning tea consisted of an apple and some sweet, packaged plastic-wrapped treat that I would hastily leave out for them on our kitchen benchtop before going to work each morning. Was I setting them up for a lifetime of bad food choices? I had read numerous stories about the obesity epidemic ruining our children and felt that this was yet another example of how I was 'failing' as a mother.

But I managed to stop my mind from racing to worst-case scenarios by doing my deep-breathing exercises. The simple mindfulness technique of thinking about your breath when you breathe in and out had become a user-friendly way for me to manage my anxiety. Breathe in for four, out for four and then you're meant to hold for four seconds. (For some reason I always got stuck with the holding part and would think too much about what would happen if I held my breath for too long!) Once my thoughts were under control, I got angry and thought, *Damn it!* (I'm not a swearer and that's as blue as my language gets.) I then decided to start Instagram posting exactly what I cooked for my family each and every night. So, that Sunday night I posted a picture of baked beans in a saucepan along with the words: *Sunday—it must be baked beans and toast for dinner* with the hashtag #craphousewife. On Monday, the picture was of six sizzling sausages in varying states of charcoal, *Today is Monday . . . Monday—sausages!* #smokealarm #craphousewife.

Each evening I revealed my lack of culinary expertise: it might have been a picture of spaghetti bolognaise, canned spaghetti, fried rice, pasta or charcoal chicken wings. The pictures became my protest, my rallying cry that I'm doing my best. Okay, I'm a crappy cook and messy 'housekeeper' but that doesn't matter. There are plenty of other things I'm good at: I love my family fiercely, I'm a loyal friend (even if I don't return phone calls), a good daughter, I'm kind and I like to laugh loudly. I'm good at wearing glittery eyeliner, online shopping, being silly with my daughters, perking up my husband, dressing up in costumes and eating chocolate in bed.

What I didn't expect from my #craphousewife posts was to find a tribe of fellow crap housewives! Now I've connected with an army of fine women who are also doing their very best in their lives to manage the demands of family, work, ageing parents, partners and friends. I love that we're sharing our pictures of mangled meals with an understanding that no one has the perfect life. We understand that those beautiful Valencia-filtered images you see on social media aren't real. Social media can be bad for your mental health, as those immaculate, fake images can make you second-guess your own life. But I'm all for sharing the realities and routine of every day. No one has the beautiful life, with the perfect career, well-behaved children and a flawless marriage.

I'm weary of the nonsense message about women 'having it all'. (We never ask men if they can 'have it all' — but that's a whole other book.) What does 'having it all' mean anyway? For me, I've discovered that I can have it all, but not at the same time. It has been impossible for me to have a career, running at a trillion miles an hour, and to be present for my family all at once. There is a time and a season for everything, and I've learnt that something always has to give to make room for what matters to you, right here, right now. And for all of us, that breaking point comes at different times and during different phases of our lives.

What I hope you get from this collection of stories is a sense of being understood and supported in the way you're leading your life. I'm far from having all of the answers but I do know that sharing our stories of failure, triumph and joy is a way of feeling connected. This book is my way of showing there is no one-size-fits-all way to be the best mother, wife, friend and daughter. Laughter is intrinsic to my DNA and I never like to take myself too seriously, even though my dear husband wishes I would tone down my craziness sometimes!

However, over the years I have become more outlandish in my style and that is why I'm drawn to the trailblazing work of the comedian Phyllis Diller. This mother of six children, who had a cackling laugh and wore flamboyant costumes, embraced stand-up comedy in the fifties. At the heart of her routines was sending up her lack of 'good' housewife skills. She is my spirit animal.

My wish for this little book is that you can find some sparkle, light and sprinklings of fairy dust as you navigate your own not-so-perfect but glorious life! Plus, I've included some of my favourite and easiest recipes that I regularly feed my family. I'm always looking for nightly meal inspiration as there is nothing more soul-destroying than cooking meals that no one will eat! And the recipes I've included are crowd pleasers (mind you—Peter now gets his meals from a food delivery service). Crap housewives of the world unite!

SPAGHETTI BOLOGNAISE

We have spag bol at least once a week! I can't think of a family
that doesn't rely on this Italian favourite on a semi-regular basis.
Sometimes I'll use the leftover mince to make a shepherd's pie
or nachos or lasagne. Mince is a highly underrated meat!

Ingredients
500 g beef mince
1 jar of pasta sauce
1 jar of canned tomatoes
1 packet of spaghetti (we like to mix it up with pasta shells
    or bow tie pasta)
as much or as little grated parmesan cheese as you like

Method
Heat frypan over a medium heat, add mince, stirring occasionally
while it's cooking. Once it's cooked, drain off any excess fat, add jar
of pasta sauce and stir it through with the canned tomatoes. Turn
heat down to low and let it simmer for 20 minutes. This cooking
time varies for me depending on how hungry my girls are!

Meanwhile, bring a pot of water to the boil, add your pasta and
cook for 8–10 minutes.

Serve with grated parmesan cheese, crusty bread and salad.

Success rate

Three out of four family members love this. My daughters have been eating spag bol since they were tiny. I remember using a Bamix to mush it up for them when they first started on solid food. At the time, I was a little obsessed with pureeing everything in sight. However, Peter fell out of love with this meal a long time ago and he never, ever wants to see another bowl of spaghetti bolognaise.

1

Reinvention

If it costs you your peace, it's too expensive.

UNKNOWN

Little splashes of pool water forced my eyes open to stare up at the soft, afternoon sunshine. These flicks of cool water were coming from the graceful kicks of my youngest daughter. She had been pushing me and the giant inflatable pizza that I was lying on, around the blue, slippery, tiled swimming pool.

'Guess who, Mummy?' laughed my eight-year-old.

'No idea. Who is this mystery mermaid taking me and my pizza on a tour?'

The pair of us kept talking nonsense and laughing loudly into the lazy sky. A dragonfly with transparent silver wings buzzed near the pool surface.

'Remember this, Jessica,' whispered my heart. 'You are happy, right here, right now.'

Later that day, I proudly declared to my husband, Peter, that I was leaving my television job. The pair of us were talking, while we watched our daughters twirl around in the shallow surf on the edge of Khao Lak beach in Thailand. He was used to my haphazard plans and took a long sip of his happy-hour gin and tonic, digging his toes into the sand, before responding.

'Pussycat, what will you do? I know you. You like to have a project and I worry that you'll get bored. You're going to miss the attention from being on the television. Remember how long you waited to have a job like *Studio 10?*'

Peter was right. I was doing a job that I loved and in the rough-and-tumble world of media, I'd finally landed the right job at the right time. And I'd had my fair share of jobs, having worked for all the commercial television networks in Australia. The only places still left for me to work at were the public broadcasters, ABC and SBS. I had been working on *Studio 10*, the morning tele-vision chat show on Network Ten, for four years. The role was like returning home for me as I had spent an early part of my broadcasting career reading for the *Five O'Clock*

News on Ten. Now I had found my niche on a panel chat show and it was quite simply the best television job I'd ever had.

Throwing off my news-presenter impartiality, I relished the opportunity to debate the big and little topics of the day on *Studio 10*. For the first time, I was truly myself on the telly and it meant snorting while I laughed without any bosses telling me to rein it in (as I had been told to do at another network). I could also passionately debate the issues that made my bleeding heart ache: topics like mental health, refugees, Indigenous issues and sexism.

#CRAPHOUSEWIFE

As a teenager I used to hand out 'How to vote' cards for the Labor Party, in one of the ritziest, most monied parts of Sydney. Walking down the queue of voters and clutching my Labor literature, women wearing ropes of Paspaley pearls and Salvatore Ferragamo flats would try to counsel me.

'What is a nice girl like you doing handing out pamphlets for these communists?'

I explained that I was a proud member of Young Labor and urged them to support the party. Somehow I don't imagine I converted many of these silvertails and silver foxes!

Over 30 years later, that 'nice girl' was no longer handing out political pamphlets and had become more of a self-declared champagne socialist or limousine leftie. My mother could never work out where I got my expensive tastes from as she'd never been taken in by fancy clothes or shoes. She preferred to spend her hard-earned money on books or tickets for gloomy art-house movies. However, what I did inherit from her (and my father) is a passion for social justice and community.

#CRAPHOUSEWIFE

Five mornings a week I had the privilege of sitting alongside my friends, journalists Sarah Harris and Joe Hildebrand, media icon Ita Buttrose and showbiz royalty Denise Drysdale (Neesy). We would also on occasion be joined by guest panellists, who guaranteed that the conversation remained unpredictable and entertaining. Everything I debated on the show came from my heart and there were moments when it was tough to put myself 'out there', day after day.

Frequently I was the lone voice on issues, a badge I sported proudly, but at times it did wear me down. One such time was when radio host Steve Price, Joe, Ita and I were talking about the behaviour of the then Greens Senator Larissa Waters who had been forced to resign from federal parliament because of her Canadian citizenship. Following is some of our discussion:

'I think she's a terrific senator and she's done a lot of good,' I said.

'What has she done, exactly?' asked Joe.

'She made a mistake and I think it's our loss that she's no longer in the parliament,' I said.

'Why? What's she done, apart from breastfeed her baby in the Senate?' replied Steve Price.

'But you say that in a very patronising way, Steve,' I said.

'But what has she done?' asked Joe.

'Again Joe, don't be a smart-arse!' I replied.

'All we're asking is what has she done? You said she's done a lot. Just tell us what she's done instead of attacking the question,' Joe persisted.

'Sometimes it's very difficult to respond to a question when you sound like you're an expert on everything,' I said.

Okay, calling Joe a smart-arse wasn't my finest moment and I wished I'd been more articulate. In my dressing-room after that show I burst into tears, exhausted and angry at myself that I hadn't made my point clearly. It was never simply 'sport' for me and such exchanges would eat away at my stamina and confidence. At other times, a sharp word from Ita or an arch of one of her immaculate eyebrows would be enough to wear me down. Of course it was the nature of the show that we would at times clash over our different opinions. It was entertaining to watch and it would have been terribly boring if we had agreed on everything, all the time! Rationally, I knew that but when I was tired it was hard not to take such exchanges personally.

Another time, notorious British attention-seeker and conservative Milo Yiannopoulos came on the show to promote his upcoming speaking tour in Australia. During the interview I made it clear I didn't support his views and was a 'proud feminist'.

'That's okay, I'm sure they'll cure you soon. There's a chemotherapy for that,' replied Milo.

'No, no, no,' I said. 'Everyone is entitled to a view but you seem to stir up hate for the sake of it, because you want to provoke.'

Our interview continued along the same vein and later that day, he uploaded the interview to his YouTube channel under the headline: 'Milo slays half-bald feminist.'

Over the years I've had my share of nasty comments and I understood that a degree of criticism comes with being in the public eye. Most of that I could handle; however, what is never excusable is violent, misogynistic trolling. After the incident with Milo I dealt with the vile comments by blocking users' accounts. It's incredibly satisfying pushing that block button and each time I did that, I was reminded of the wise words of my late grandmother: 'Don't let them take your peace, Jessica.'

But my time on the show wasn't all about blocking trolls. There were many, many moments of simple joy and silliness that made it so special. During high school I had enjoyed decorating T-shirts, knitting jumpers and creating costumes that I would sell at the Paddington Market in Sydney. Now I was again able to indulge in my flamboyant flair for creating a costume for our Halloween shows. One year I decided to dress up as a crazy cat lady! My daughters had generously let me borrow their precious cuddly cat toys, which I stitched haphazardly all over my pink chenille dressing gown. Some of the stuffed cats needed some large safety pins through their paws to secure them snuggly onto my shoulders. The look was completed with hair rollers, Dame Edna–style sunglasses and my own leopard-print pyjama pants.

Another time I got out the needle and thread was for yet another Halloween show. This time, my boss let me dress as a fart! He had been very accommodating with my costume requests. And I'll never forget the look of horror on Ita's face when I surprised the panel with my explosive get-up.

'I've always wanted to be a fart,' I told the audience and panel, laughing. 'It's a dream come true!'

I sounded slightly out of breath after running onto the set at the last moment after ditching the white terry towelling bathrobe that had been covering my outfit.

Much of the night before I had sat up in bed, hand-stitching white, brown and green tulle, which I had bought on special from Spotlight, onto my eldest daughter's old school headband. Once I had finished the headgear, it was time to sew the leftover layers of tulle onto a beige singlet. My stretchy white pants would complete the costume. Peter had given up asking me to turn off the bedside lamp and exclaimed that I was getting more eccentric the older I got! And that is the joy of ageing. I was caring less and less about what people thought of me and my methods of 'self-expression'.

Luckily, I am married to a man who has bucketloads of common sense, and so I did listen to his advice when he cautioned me to wait before I resigned from my television job. And my husband (who is frequently right) knew that I was an attention-seeker and that I did enjoy the notoriety that came from working in the media. Even though I knew I was more than my job title, there was satisfaction and vanity that came from 'being somebody'. I'm ashamed to admit that the validation of being on *Studio 10* puffed up my self-esteem. Despite my 'worthiness', I knew I could also be shallow and enjoyed that my 'celebrity' meant I could get a good seat in a restaurant and a discount from my favourite designers.

#CRAPHOUSEWIFE

Returning to work in January after enjoying being off in a lovely holiday bubble in Thailand, I set myself the goal of working for another year on *Studio 10*. For some reason, I arbitrarily came up with the target of doing twelve more months at work but I'm not sure who I was trying to impress with that decision. Fast-forward a few months and that whisper of my heart that I heard on holidays was no longer sounding soft and gentle. Instead, it was getting louder and more insistent: 'Just keep going.' 'How many more sleeps until the weekend?' 'How many weeks until our next break?' 'What about school holidays? How do I stop feeling guilty, keep our girls happy while we both juggle our work schedules?' 'Should I ask work if I can get the morning off to go to the swimming carnival? Or should I wait until the Mother's Day breakfast and ask for that morning off instead?'

I didn't like the person I was morphing into— someone who was sleepwalking through the days after getting up early for work after another night of too-little sleep. Although I had managed to throw out that Super Woman nonsense years before, I still couldn't wipe away the mother guilt that seeped deeply into my soft, mushy heart. Now that my daughters were getting older, I realised they needed me more than ever. I couldn't ignore my life's greatest work—being the best mother for them.

When my daughters were tiny I used to love the freedom of sneaking out to work like a ninja, as the sun was just waking up, happy that my little family were still sound asleep and dreaming heavily. Smiling as I saw the lilac morning light when I opened the front door, I'd quickly check that my handbag was crammed with all that I needed for the day.

'Favourite pink lipstick, check. Padded bra, check. Shorthand notebook, check. Different pair of undies with no VPL (in case I would be wearing a tight dress on the telly), check.'

My heart would sing as I'd hear the cheeky kookaburras clearing their throats while quietly closing my car door, ready for a new day. I hadn't realised how lost I had been without a paid job. A job that had helped my brainwaves rediscover their silver, zapping rhythms independent of controlled-crying routines, dirty sandpits, playground politics and endless routine. Without realising, I had allowed my identity as a woman to become secondary to my identity as a mother, nurturer and keeper of everyone else's happiness. At last I felt like myself again and I had missed her.

But isn't there always a rub when something is too good to be true? Alas, the sting in the tail—the obstacle that used to break my stride when my girls were small—was mother guilt. Of course I realised how useless guilt is as an emotion but it can be hard to ignore its destructive force when you're tired, not able to do canteen duty, or have forgotten to get the schoolbags out of the boot of the car from the night before. Initially, I used to worry that I was depriving my girls because I wasn't with them 24/7. However, I've learnt that it doesn't matter how much time you spend with your kids, they always want more!

I'm still guilty of trying to make up for that void with bribery, corruption and then the spoiling that I can't resist when it comes to the greatest loves of my life. I'm fearful of the terrible consequences that come from relying on such shallow tools to soothe my feelings of not being a good enough mum. Are you also weary of the endless studies about how soft parenting styles are turning our kids into juvenile delinquents? I try not to read them, and I won't read them. Tough love has never been my style. But there goes that voice again, that I'm turning my daughters into spoilt brats who have no boundaries and believe the world owes them.

Of course, mothers are to blame for all that is wrong with their children—it is never the fathers . . . And hey, I spent years and many hours dealing with 'mother issues' by seeing a therapist each fortnight. Rarely do we hear about how 'father issues' have ruined someone's life forever. We need to take the pressure off ourselves and our mothering skills. We are good enough!

But I do know I am a soft touch and my daughters can smell my vulnerability. I can still clearly remember a time when my youngest was still at day care and I'd just returned to full-time work.

'Mummy, will you pick me up early from preschool today?' asked Giselle.

'Sure, I'll get you just before your afternoon tea and we can have some special time before we pick up Allegra from school,' I replied.

After bolting from work and doing a record-breaking dash around the supermarket, I made it to the preschool gates just as the class was sitting down on their miniature plastic chairs to start on their cheese and fruit snacks. I crouched down next to my cherubic child.

'I'm NOT ready to go yet!'

'But, but you wanted me to pick you up early . . .'

'This is my favourite part of the day. I'm NOT going yet.'

I pulled up one of the spare weeny plastic chairs and squished next to my indignant daughter, waiting for her to be 'ready' to leave day care. *I'm a bad mother, bad mother . . . she would rather be here than spending time with me,* I told myself. But my husband doesn't have the same inner dialogue. I don't know any men who do. So why do we do it?

A girlfriend of mine buys her sons LEGO, she calls it LEGO guilt. If she feels like she has had an especially busy week at work, a quick trip to Kmart is compulsory. The shopping bags sit on the kitchen benchtop in time for her sons to discover their treats once they're home from school. Her boys don't ask or whinge to get the latest LEGO—my friend simply does it to make herself feel better.

I do the same. Not with LEGO, but I like to have treats for my girls most afternoons. Not top-shelf toys, but sometimes a punnet of fresh raspberries, Vegemite scrolls, colouring-in books, textas, Bubble O' Bill ice-creams and the occasional Barbie. Why? Because I put this ridiculous pressure on myself and won't back my mothering skills. However, I'm getting better at realising that I'm a good mum. Actually, I'm a marvellous mother; I'm fun, honest, patient and always up for a chat. And I love my girls more than the number of shining stars in our galaxy and beyond.

#CRAPHOUSEWIFE

My eldest daughter, Allegra, aged eleven, had been setting her alarm so she could wake up early with me before I left for work each morning. Something she had been doing for the past year. The pair of us would chat in the dark together, as the morning star faded from the sky. I'd pat her honey-blonde hair while she lay stretched across my lap, snuggled under the fluffy, fuchsia-pink mohair rug.

One morning she asked: 'Mummy, can I have a play date this afternoon?'

'No, my darling.'

'Why not? I really want to have Rosie around!'

'Um, well, we're busy . . .'

'What about the weekend? Please, Mum. Mummy?'

The thought of looking after any more children left me weary. I was too tired, I was always too tired. When I was growing up, we never had organised play dates so the idea was already foreign to me. Something had to shift as I realised I was saying 'no' too much, saying 'no' to what mattered, in contrast to saying 'yes' to those professional commitments. I had always liked to think of myself as a 'yes' girl when it came to chasing fun, but now that was happening less and less.

Working meant I was 'on' for those three and a half hours of live television each day. Regardless of my mood, the thrill of debating, discussing and laughing about the issues of the day with my colleagues kept me showing up every morning. The comedown from each 'perform-ance' would hit me harder as I became more tired. I was surviving on adrenaline, then propping myself up with rosé of a Friday night to take the edge off my buzzy brain. I knew I was drinking too much but it had become a prop to get me through the week.

The whisper was becoming more urgent: 'Jessica, what are you doing? Why are you doing this? You're not happy.'

You may be thinking, *What an ungrateful and whingy woman. You have a wonderful job, a great marriage, gorgeous kids. What do you have to be tired and precious about?* And you're right, I do have a good life. I knew I was lucky but I also knew that if I kept going along this path I'd become resentful and cruel to the people I love the most. Each afternoon I was becoming more and more the 'shouty mummy'. Sure, we all have our bad days but it seemed like more of my days were ending with me feeling exhausted and empty.

It didn't matter that my daughters raised their eyebrows and giggled at me, wondering what had happened to their 'funny' mummy. I had thought having a Christmas break would leave me re-energised and ready to take on another year of early starts on television. But I had to listen to my heart. (Remember, I was a teenager of the eighties and that Roxette song is still one of my favourites!) Like any big decision we make in our lives, there are always moments of fear when we consider making a big change.

Leaps of faith have been a constant in my life. I'd always rather risk something and live a little dangerously instead of leading a small, safe life full of regret. I left home aged seventeen, to study in a small country town in western New South Wales. Then, there was a year of 'modelling' in Germany, starring in camping and skiwear catalogues. Probably more of that year was spent dancing on the tops of bars rather than making bedroom eyes at the camera lens.

I then returned to Australia, finished my media degree and moved around the country for jobs in journalism. Some of those jobs worked out better than others! Hello, the *Today* show . . . However, I don't regret anything. In the past I'd been brave, so it was now time to rediscover that bold part of myself and make a change.

My patient husband and long-suffering friends had listened to me dithering over my decision for long enough. The time for talking was over and it was time to listen to my inner voice, my intuition. And to listen, really listen, to those softly, softly moments when the beat of your heart whispers louder than the rational, so-called sensible part of your brain. What helped me to reach my decision was reading some books that had serendipitously arrived in my post-office box. These included *Slow* by Brooke McAlary, as well as Meshel Laurie's *Buddhism for the Unbelievably Busy*. It's bizarre how books, people and friends will appear when you need to read/hear/understand a moment in your life. I've never been a religious soul; however, I do believe in a higher spirit keeping us spinning on the right axis for most of the time.

Now, the right thing for me was to slow down so I could feel the pull of my heartstrings. The heartstrings that had tightly bound me to my babies were now a little looser but were being tugged by the emotional demands of their tween years and the emotionally fraught teenage years that lay ahead. I had been a nightmare teenager and my stubborn streak, which works for me now, didn't make me an easy person to get along with. I recognised that same strength and determination in my girls and wanted to be present to help them navigate the hormones and the occasional horribleness of being a girl growing into a young woman.

What do I mean by being present? Mindfulness and being in the moment are terms that are increasingly thrown around counselling sessions, workplaces and classrooms. And it's a relief to learn that more and more people are looking for ways to lead a meaningful life. But sometimes that search can be stressful! Stripping it back to basics, for me being present means being emotionally present. My daughters needed me and I needed them. And I knew just how lucky I was to have this choice.

The morning I announced that I was leaving Channel Ten, I told Allegra how nervous I was about sharing the news with my colleagues and viewers in a few hours' time. Kissing the top of her head and marvelling at her loveliness, I asked her what she thought about my decision.

'A billion times happier Mummy,' she said.

And I couldn't argue with that.

Nor could I ignore the bright, beaming smile of my youngest daughter, Giselle. Now I can take her to school each morning. I had never been able to do that before as she started school just after I'd returned to full-time work. Now we hold hands—my big hand holds her hot, little hand that reaches for mine the moment we get out of the car.

'What do you call a pile of cats?' I asked.

'Oh, Mummy. It's called a meow-tain. And that's a lame joke!'

'Yes, I know, that's a shocker of a joke. How about I sing you a song! I promise it won't be embarrass-SING,' I replied, cracking myself up.

'Mum, that is not funny!' Giselle said. 'You know I love you taking me to school, though.'

'Oh, my baby bear. I *love* taking you to school, my darling heart.'

It is never simply a choice between career and family. Life is never black and white, regardless of how much easier that would make it when it comes to all the big and little decisions that make up the wonder of our lives. Ask anyone, and family always comes first. Sometimes you have to lean in more to your family or to your career, depending on what stage you're at in your life. Right now, I'm leaning in hard for my girls and my man. This isn't old-fashioned; I'm a proud feminist and my brand of feminism is all about supporting the different choices that we can and should have as women. Who knows what lies ahead? But I can promise you that some things won't change because this crap housewife won't be putting away the laundry any time soon!

BREKKIE BRUSCHETTA

This is from the chef Ash Pollard, and it features in her *Eat Me* e-cookbook. It ticks all of my boxes: quick, easy and with minimal opportunities to stuff it up!

Ingredients
1 packet of bacon
an egg for each person
one punnet of cherry tomatoes
a handful of fresh basil leaves
a generous splash of olive oil
a generous splash of balsamic vinegar
as much butter as you like to fry your eggs
one loaf of crusty bread

Method
In one frypan cook the bacon. While this is cooking, slice the cherry tomatoes in half, then put them in a bowl with shredded basil leaves.

Ash also suggests slicing up 1 Spanish onion and adding it to the bowl (I left this out as I get bad onion breath).

Drizzle with olive oil, balsamic vinegar and season with salt and pepper.

In another frypan, melt some butter, and lightly toast your crusty bread in one corner of the pan, take the bread out, and crack some eggs and fry them how you like them.

Once everything is cooked, first put your cherry tomatoes mix on the bread, then the rasher of bacon and top with the fried egg. Drizzle some extra balsamic if you want. Season with salt and pepper.

Success rate

Three out of four family members loved this! Peter ate his in about three seconds, Allegra ate hers and told me I should be on *MasterChef* and Giselle just ate the bacon on its own!

2

Cooking

Be yourself. Everyone else is already taken.

OSCAR WILDE

I am not a cook. Beep, beep, beep, beeeeeeep. The ear-splitting sounds of the kitchen smoke alarm go off with such frequency in our house that even our three cats, Daisy, Alfie and Violet, cannot be roused from their sleeping, snuggly spot next to the mismatched socks on the dining-room table. Our cats still won't budge even as I try to bang the corner of the smoke alarm sensor with the broomstick to turn it off before the alarm company rings to check if they need to send the fire brigade!

When we bought the small French-imitation round table, I had visions of my daughters and me sitting around it, sharing a delicious roast dinner. The chook would be cooked to golden perfection, alongside perfectly crunchy roast potatoes and bright-green, glossy beans. There would also be homemade gravy without lumps, full of flavour and kept warm in a white porcelain jug on the table.

The television and any electronic devices would be turned off without an argument. So the only sound, after we chewed our tender meat with our mouths closed, would be thoughtful observations from my daughters and conversation that they volunteered without any badgering from me about what they did at school. Their dad's dinner would be plated up ready to be gently heated once he got home from reading the news on television. And by the time he got home, the girls would be upstairs, bathed and in their pyjamas, reading quietly in bed! Clearly this is not my reality. Is it any family's reality?

Our dining table gets so little regular use, apart from being the cats' day/night beds, it has become a dumping ground for clean baskets of laundry, piles of yellow Post-it notes, blunt lead pencils and texta lids looking for a home. When I was growing up, my sisters and I rarely ate dinner in front of the television and sometimes I worry that my own daughters are developing antisocial habits since we don't often all sit together at the table for mealtimes. But when everyone's weary after a long day, the last thing I want to do is more nagging to get them to sit at the table. Instead, the pair of them are usually perched on stools around our kitchen benchtop, while I dance near the sink entertaining them.

'Mum, you're sooooo embarrassing,' said Allegra.

Oh, this was pure delight to my ears, so I started doing my next party trick, pretending to walk down an escalator on the other side of the kitchen bench.

'MUM!' said my eldest, while her younger sister laughed and laughed.

The phone rang, interrupting my Logie-worthy performance.

'Petee, shouldn't you be getting ready for the news?'

'I'm just going down to the studio now but I wanted to say a quick hello!'

'Hello, Petee!'

'What's for dinner, Pussycat?' I could hear the hope in his voice.

'It's chicken wings!'

'Pussycat, you know I don't like chicken wings. Even when I was little I hated them!'

'But it isn't pasta, Petee! You keep telling me you want to stay off the carbs!'

#CRAPHOUSEWIFE

Marinated chicken wings have become a welcome addition to my weekly dinner menu. Spaghetti bolognaise is always my number one choice but I know I need to keep mixing things up a little. As a small girl I used to love marinated chicken wings and I know my daughters will enjoy them too. Earlier in the day, I phoned one of my capable, organised banker friends for the 'recipe'.

'What goes in a honey and soy marinade for chicken wings?' I asked, hearing the buzz of her busy office in the background.

There is the briefest of pauses on the other end of the phone before she says, 'Honey AND soy!'

'Yes, but how much of each? I need specifics!'

'Put in the same amount of each and add a slurp of vegetable oil.'

Yes, it's that easy!

Another sweet piece of cooking wisdom that I've picked up from an equally capable friend, the darling Denise Drysdale, has been panko crumbs. What is a panko? It's Japanese-style breadcrumbs, made from bread without crusts. Why panko? Well, according to Neesy they don't absorb as much grease as standard breadcrumbs, making them super crunchy. And she's right—these golden, crispy crumbs have elevated schnitzels, cutlets and rissoles into meals that my whole family will eat.

Another game changer for my cooking is yet another piece of invaluable advice from Neesy: 'God Almighty, turn the hotplate down. You have everything up too high!'

And she was right (I'd asked her for the best way to stop burning my food).

#CRAPHOUSEWIFE

My husband is well aware of my culinary and domestic shortcomings and he didn't marry me for my abilities in the kitchen. Besides, I often tell him he's welcome to take over the cooking duties but, like me, he doesn't enjoy it. This means he has to deal with what I serve up each night. He's not on Instagram so many of his younger newsroom colleagues who follow my #craphousewife posts will let him know what he's having for dinner. One of his favourite producers, who talks to him through an earpiece during his hourly news bulletin, will tell him during an ad break how his evening meal is looking.

'Pete, those chicken wings aren't looking good tonight! It's more charcoal than marinade. I think you should be picking up some Thai takeaway on the way home!' says the producer.

At least my husband has been forewarned.

However, the girls and I are oblivious to this warning as we continue with our nightly routine.

'Oh look, there's your daddy on the television. Let's say goodnight!' I say to the girls.

The three of us wave at the telly and I tell them how handsome their father looks.

'Mum, that's disgusting!' says my eldest daughter.

'Allegra, all I'm saying is that your daddy is handsome. And I love him!'

And all my soon-to-be-teenage daughter can do is roll her eyes at her crazy mother.

#CRAPHOUSEWIFE

Apart from my vaudeville act, our evening routine usually involves me cooking while I try to supervise homework of varying degrees of difficulty. Since timing has never been my strong point, dinnertime suddenly creeps up and I find myself rushing around, turning up the oven or the hot-plate too high (despite Neesy's instructions) because of my delusion this will make it cook faster. And when I've got a spare second, I'll bolt upstairs to the toilet since I've forgotten to go all day.

'Mum, have you got a pencil?' yelled Allegra from the bottom of the stairs.

'I put a pile of them next to the green paint tube on the table yesterday,' I shouted from the bathroom.

Why is it that all the questions start once you're in the bathroom? Or on the phone?

'What?'

'I'm not shouting! Come up here and ask!' I shouted.

'I need a pencil for my homework. And I need you to come downstairs now and help me.'

'Have you looked properly? I'm sure there are some right next to the polystyrene green peas that I painted for Giselle's *Princess and the Pea* Book Week costume!'

'What?' shouted Allegra.

Quickly, I'm back downstairs, waving a selection of HB lead pencils that are exactly where I said they would be: on the table.

'Mum, can't you just tell me the answers?'

'No, it's not my homework. It's yours . . .'

'But I don't understand what past perfect tense means?'

'Umm, well.' I'm tempted to tell my daughter that I have no idea what it is either. Thank goodness for Google when it comes to those tricky homework questions. During my time at school we didn't learn any rules about grammar, as the English syllabus had focused on the concept that it was correct if it 'sounded' or 'looked' right. (Not sur-prisingly, this teaching approach meant I failed grammar during the first year of my journalism degree.)

And even though I did three-unit maths in high school, I was as much in the dark about my youngest daughter's maths homework too. I had no idea how to explain the number line and placement value they now use at school to teach addition, subtraction and fractions.

'Mumma, I don't get this Mathletics question,' said Giselle, as she pointed at the downloaded maths program on my laptop that she uses for her homework.

'Alright, let's see. Oh, it's fractions!' I replied.

'I don't understand why I keep getting the wrong answer.'

'Imagine that it's a whole pizza and then you cut the pizza in half, and then you cut it again to share with your daddy,' I said hopefully.

'Mumma, you're weird. You don't make any sense! Can't you just do it for me?' asked Giselle.

'No, I can't just do it!' I said, and then muttered under my breath, 'Homework is such a waste of time.'

More and more I find I'm talking out loud to myself and I also find myself sighing loudly when I sit down or get up. I think it's a part of getting older. But back to homework, why is it such a punish? Haven't we parents (and kids) got enough to do without filling our afternoons with even more work? Besides, I think it's the teacher's way of working out how smart the parents are!

'Muuuuum, what's for dinner tonight? Can we have hot chips?' asked Allegra. 'Please can we have hot chips? I love hot chips.' Her persistent voice stopped my internal monologue about homework.

'It's chicken wings tonight,' I replied, trying to sound upbeat.

My daughter recognised that slight waiver in my voice and tried again with her questions.

'What about pizza?'

I knew I should have used a different food to describe fractions to her sister.

'No—you know that's our Friday night treat.'

'Can I eat dinner in front of the telly? We could watch some of those YouTube *Miranda Sings* videos?'

'We'll see.'

I'm hesitating, aware that some mindless videos will give me twenty minutes' freedom from a cross-examination about why I believe Cardi B is inappropriate and not a good role model for young girls.

'That means yes! And when can I get my ears pierced? It's not fair I have to wait until I'm twelve.'

#CRAPHOUSEWIFE

Although I keep my cooking repertoire simple with spaghetti bolognaise, chicken wings, schnitzel and sausages, there have been occasions when I will experiment and try something new. When I shared the *Studio 10* desk with comedian Mikey Robins, he would always talk to me about restaurants and recipes in the commercial breaks. He recommended an 'easy' Jamie Oliver recipe that involved sausages. It sounded good and I knew that both my husband and daughters love sausages. Unfortunately, though, I again got distracted during the cooking process.

'What on earth is this, Pussycat?' asked my husband, as I dished up his meal.

'I call it sausage surprise, Petee!'

'It's certainly a surprise!'

'Come on, try it. And there's no pasta in it,' I said, as I spooned out sliced-up sausages, cherry tomatoes and garlic.

It's unusual for the two of us to sit during the week and eat a meal together, even if it's called 'sausage surprise'. Typically, Peter will come home from work and I'll be wrangling our daughters in or out of the bath. There's plenty of chaos, noise and laughter.

'Pussycat, why can't we be a normal family?'

I'm not sure where my husband gets his ideas about 'normal' families, given he grew up in a noisy, loving big family. Perhaps it's just wishful thinking on his part that he'll have a quiet, drama-free night at home.

'Surely other families don't carry on like this!' he said as he walked upstairs, hearing me ask, ask and ask the girls to please clean their teeth.

'My darling, this is normal!' I shouted, while he retreated back downstairs to zap his dinner in the microwave.

#CRAPHOUSEWIFE

Another time, when I was in the mood to mix things up, I cooked up a lamb roast with herb and tomato stuffing. The only reason I tackled this dish was because it was one of those supermarket-prepared meals. All that was left for me to do was follow the cooking instructions on the Jamie Oliver packet. Foolproof, or so I thought. Everyone ate up their roast dinner happily and I was feeling rather chuffed with myself. However, my heart skipped a beat when I was clearing up the kitchen bench and I noticed a small piece of rectangular plastic packaging that was still attached to the leftover roast. I didn't say a word to my husband or girls about my suspicious discovery.

'Petee, what did you think of the roast?' I asked, scraping the leftovers into the rubbish bin.

'Pussycat, it was delicious! One of your better meals,' he replied, wiping down the benchtop.

Quickly, I snuck into the bathroom to ring my youngest sister, Claudia, who is a professional chef, about my cooking mishap. She has always been my go-to girl when I had questions about use-by dates of food, whether something was cooked, or how long I could keep a barbecued chook in the fridge.

'Claudo, I'm worried I've poisoned the family?' I murmured into the phone.

'WHAT?' replied my sister.

'Ssshh, don't shout!' I said, not wanting to be sprung hiding in the bathroom. 'I cooked one of those Jamie Oliver meals and I cooked it with some of the packaging.'

'Oh . . . kay, don't tell me how you managed not to see the plastic packaging. But don't worry, there's nothing in those squares. Everyone will be fine and the high cooking temperature would have killed off any nasties anyway!'

And guess what? My little sister was spot on: no one got sick and I didn't need to reveal my near-poisoning fears to my husband and children! Claudia is a wonderful cook and a Jamie Oliver expert, having worked for him at The River Cafe in London. She has also run other restaurants in London and Sydney. Apart from being a world-class chef, she has also been helping me, on the sly, in the kitchen for years.

Before I became an out-and-proud crap housewife I used to pretend to be a good cook by serving up what Claudia had prepared for me! I'm ashamed to admit to 'hosting' dinner parties and serving up menus cooked solely by my sister. I would proudly pretend to our guests that I had whipped up the bruschetta entree, the main course of Moroccan lamb tagine served alongside couscous tossed gently with black currants. My sister would drop all of the dishes around earlier in the day and all I had to do was heat them up according to her written instructions. The main contribution I made to the meal was scooping the Sara Lee French vanilla ice-cream out of the tub and serving it with strawberries for dessert.

One persistent guest almost exposed my ruse one evening when she wouldn't let up on her request for the lamb tagine recipe. Thankfully, she didn't notice the deep reddening of my face thanks to the pinot grigio we'd all been enjoying with our delicious meal. Shrugging my shoulders, I laughed loudly, while my honest husband became engrossed in rearranging the salt and pepper shakers on the table,

'I don't remember exactly. I just threw a few bits and pieces together.'

But my dinner companion wasn't satisfied with that explanation: 'You must tell me what spices you used. Was it paprika or turmeric?'

The next day I asked my sister to write out the recipe for me and I emailed it to my dinner guest. That was the last time I pretended to be someone that I wasn't as I realised the stupidity and exhaustion that came from pretending to know the difference between turmeric and paprika. All that wasted time pretending to be one of those people who can whip up a meal with only a few ingredients in the fridge, along with a drizzle—or is it grizzle?—of olive oil and some casually torn basil leaves.

It has been a lifetime since we hosted a fancy dinner party. Entertaining guests fills me with anxiety and I've always marvelled at people who can effortlessly host a dinner. All of us have different skill sets and I'm over pretending that one of mine is being great around the home. Now, when we invite friends around, I get Peter to be in charge of the barbecue and I make a giant green salad and serve it with crusty French bread. For dessert, there are Magnum ice-creams and lemonade icy poles in the freezer.

#CRAPHOUSEWIFE

Clearly, Nigella Lawson has nothing to fear from me. At a young age I managed to tangle my long hair in the egg beaters while trying to bake a cake for the tuck-shop fundraiser. Since then my baking and cooking skills haven't improved much. When I recently interviewed the real-life 'domestic goddess', Nigella was generous enough to critique my cooking. I put up a series of pictures of my meals that I'd posted on Instagram. The first one was hamburger patties. They didn't look that great in the picture but Nigella kindly told me they didn't need 'rescuing' as hamburgers were all about what 'accompaniments' you put with them.

Next up was a meal I was especially proud of as it was a radical departure from my comfort zone of spaghetti bolognaise or panko-crumbed schnitzel. My photo was of a bright, colourful salad with not a tinge of charcoal in sight. It was an easy recipe from *MasterChef* finalist Justine Schofield. I'm a big fan of her easy, no-fuss style of cooking.

'Tuna Niçoise salad . . . is that rice in there?' Nigella asked curiously.

'Yes it is,' I replied.

'Yeeees . . .'

'Is rice okay?' I said.

'Someone from Nice might disagree with you. But when you make your food you're entitled to make it as you'd like it. [You're saying:] "It's my voice and my taste."'

Now I have clearly found my voice about my lack of domesticity. Who was I trying to impress with my 'ability' to cook, do maths homework and get my children to stay in their beds each night? We aren't faultless and it's exhausting pretending to the wider world that we have it together all the time. Life with kids can be messy, tedious and wonderful. So why did I need to keep pretending that I was always spick and span?

#CRAPHOUSEWIFE

My daughters love what I cook, even if my husband isn't quite so effusive in his praise. Now he gets his meals delivered as part of a dinner delivery service but every now and then I do catch him looking longingly at my spaghetti bolognaise. Although he's not a fan of the mince, he does love carbohydrates and I know he still wants some of the pasta! But he's just weary of the weekly occurrence of spag bol in my cooking repertoire.

Recently, I was close to tears of joy at our local Chinese restaurant while Peter, my daughters and I munched spring rolls and chicken fried rice. And it wasn't only because I had a night off cooking.

'Mummy, this isn't as good as what you cook! You should be a master chef!' said Allegra.

Other evenings, Giselle enjoys helping me crumb our schnitzels, stir the jar of pasta sauce into the mince, or peel the potatoes for the mash.

'Mumma, you're a great cook!' she tells me.

And that, my beauties, is good enough for me.

SCHNITZEL

The panko crumb has changed my life! Since my darling friend Denise Drysdale introduced me to the wonders of the panko, I now try to crumb everything (apart from my husband and the cats). I've found that kids will eat anything smothered in crumbs.

Ingredients
chicken/veal schnitzel from the supermarket or butcher
flour for coating
2 eggs
1 packet of panko crumbs
vegetable oil
butter

Method
Coat the schnitzel first in flour, then egg and finish it off with panko crumbs. The definitive Denise tip is to really use the palm of your hand to flatten the schnitzel (or lamb cutlets). I use this technique when I'm at the panko crumbing stage. It's messy but very satisfying and it makes them double in size.

Heat your frypan with oil and add some butter as well. This combination has stopped my smoke alarm from going off too often! It only takes a few minutes each side to cook your schnitzel.

Serve with mashed potato and corn, salad or coleslaw.

Success rate

Four out of four family members. This is a rarity—to cook a meal that *everyone* will eat. Packets of panko crumbs empty quickly so I always try to have a few extra ones in our pantry. Or I rely on Neesy to buy giant bags on special for me when she spots them in the supermarket.

3

Botox

Fake it until you make it.

UNKNOWN

Every couple of months I have botox. I've made that choice to have the occasional jab of toxin into my face to smooth out some frown lines and look a little less world weary. Yes, I know I'm vain but I would much rather tell you that I have needles injected into my face than come up with some nonsense about sleeping ten hours and drinking green smoothies to explain my fresher-looking complexion. There is something excruciating about reading various starlets list their 'clean-living' tips behind their immaculate visages, when it's obvious they've had some enhancement! The tips from these Glamazons include drinking hot water with a squeeze of organic lemon for brekkie, eating paleo, no sugar and drinking ten litres of macadamia milk a day. Looking immaculate does not come naturally, and for many of these stars it includes having a dermatologist on tap, botox, restylane dermafillers, fraxel laser treatment, a personalised chef, nutritionist, personal trainer, manager, housekeeper, chauffeur, stylist and oodles of cash. Lying about it does nothing to support the sisterhood. Come clean, fess up to what you get done. Or if you can't be honest, zip it and stop peddling quack theories. However, I haven't always been so confident about owning up to my own vanity.

My husband thinks it's ridiculous and my daughters look bemused when I tell them about my botox. However, without any prompting from me, the girls will give me a nudge when we're walking around our neighbourhood and they spot someone who has 'too much stuff in their face'.

'Is that a blonde Kardashian, Mummy?' asked Allegra.

'She looks like one, doesn't she?' I replied. 'And that, my darling, is what happens when you have too much surgery on your face!'

It's a balancing act I tread with my own girls as I'm open with them about the small tweaks I have done but I also talk to them about the absurd abuse of plastic surgery by some young women. My daughters aren't on social media yet but from time to time they scroll through my Instagram feed, and my eldest daughter will click the 'follow' button of all the members of the Kardashian clan. Each time, my feed is suddenly invaded by these fembots. I'll unfollow them and try to explain to Allegra why these young women are not aspirational or inspirational people. Normally, I'm willing to give anyone a chance but not the Kardashians.

'Please, Mummy. Can I get the Kylie Jenner lip kit?'

'No, she's not a good role model . . .'

'But she has her own business, she's a mum and everyone else has that lip kit!'

'So who is this "everyone?"' I asked, wondering if it's the same 'everyone' that I used to tell my own mother about when I was a teenager.

After three hours of this conversation and promises about going to bed when she's told and doing homework, I'm close to breaking point.

'The Kardashians are like Bratz dolls. I think they modelled themselves on those dolls with too-big lips, too much make-up and too-dark eyebrows!' I told my determined daughter.

'But I love Bratz dolls, Mummy! They have a passion for fashion!'

'They are tacky! And their outfits are vile, my darling.'

'But Mummy, you have some jeans that make you look like a Bratz doll!'

'Okay, okay!'

'Mum, are you listening? Are you paying attention? Are you really saying that I can have the Kylie lip kit?'

'Wait a minute!' I said. 'NO, you can't!'

I'm back to holding my nerve before going down the rabbit hole of an explanation about what first made the Kardashians famous, and why she wouldn't want to grow up to be a member of that family.

#CRAPHOUSEWIFE

Now that I'm 48 years young, I'm the most comfortable that I've ever been in my body. I've got cellulite, stretch marks and other lumpy and bumpy bits. And the marvellous part of getting older is that I don't care anymore about those silvery, snail trails on my legs, bottom and thighs.

'You have a flobby bottom,' Giselle told me recently. 'Your skin is loose and mine is tight!'

I proudly explained to Giselle that I love my bottom and every other part of my body. And I ignore Allegra's 'advice' that I could get bum implants to look like Kim Kardashian.

'My Sweet Pea, I have earnt every bit of my saggy bottom and my other wobbly and flabby bits. I love that my body is strong and that it helps me to dance, leap and carry the heavy shopping bags!'

'Mum, you're so strange . . . and what is that big, black furry thing?' asked Giselle, as I step out of the shower.

Spending any time alone in the bathroom is a distant memory.

'That, my darling, is my vagina!'

'Stop, Mum. That's revolting!' interrupted Allegra.

'No, it is not! It's beautiful. And you were born through it . . .'

'Mum, ewww . . .' said Allegra.

'It's not and you have one! And it's beautiful too!' I told my eldest daughter.

'Mum, you're crazy. And I'm just happy I was born through ICF and not that disgusting thing called sex!'

'Yes, you were born by I–V–F . . .'

While I was drying myself off with the still-damp towel that I had forgotten to hang up the night before, our chat veered towards the different ways that babies are born. It was a variation of a conversation I've been having for many years with my girls.

'Mumma, I came out of that scar?' asked Giselle, pointing at my fading caesarean scar.

'Yes, you did, my Baby Bear . . . and Allegra you came out . . .'

'Yuck, Mum, I know . . .' interrupted my eldest daughter.

Another earlier version of this talk on the topic of body parts still makes me laugh when I bring it up with my daughters. The questions had already started one day when my girls and I were driving around to see my mum.

She only lived a short distance away, but judging by the amount of stuff I'd packed, you'd think we were driving to Antartica.

Allegra was onto question number 251 and it was only 9 a.m., and I was concentrating on getting through the snarl of traffic on the way to Mum's place so wasn't listening properly to my daughter's latest query.

'Mum, does Elmo have a penis?'

'Mmmm, yes,' I answered, not thinking through the consequences. Stupidly, I thought this was the end of the discussion and we could move onto question number 252, but my inquisitive daughter had her follow-up question ready.

'Where is it?'

'It's hiding under his fur,' I said as authoritatively as I could. *Hooray, I've managed this well*, I thought to myself. But my satisfaction didn't last long. On the way home from Mum's we stopped off at the butcher.

'Mummy, does *he* have a penis?'

'Aaah, some sausages please,' I ask the butcher as my face goes the colour of Elmo's fur.

Next stop is the chemist.

'Mummy, does *she* have a penis?' Allegra continues her investigation.

'Umm, no,' I whisper.

'Why not?' she replies at full volume.

'Because she's a woman.'

'Women don't have penises?'

'No, we have vaginas . . .'

'What is your vagina for?' My daughter wasn't going to give up just yet. At least we had left the chemist and were back on the footpath so no one else could hear this part of the conversation. I was tempted to ignore her. However, as we walked home, Allegra kept asking and asking. She wore me down with her persistence.

'Mmmm, your vagina is for doing wees and it's also how you were born.'

'Did I come out of your vagina?'

'Ah, yes.'

'You're joking!'

'No, my darling, I am not.' If only I had told Allegra that Elmo was a sexless Muppet! Instead I was the muppet . . .

Even though, as my girls get older, both of them have told me it's 'disgusting' to talk about our bodies, I keep talking and talking, hoping they'll listen to some of my stories.

#CRAPHOUSEWIFE

Just like the start of the Elmo situation, often it's while we're all in the car together that we have some of our best chats.

One time, the volume on the stereo was cranked up as I did my best daggy mum dancing while the car was stopped at the traffic lights. Allegra who was sitting in the front seat simply raised her eyebrows at my attempt to do rapper hands.

'Come on, this is such a groovy song. I'm just bopping along to your music. You put this song on my iTunes.'

Just then the chorus started up again, and since the lights were taking an eternity to change, I got another chance to sing along to Iggy Azalea. I thought it was okay for my daughter to listen to Amethyst Amelia Kelly as she's a hard-working, hippy girl, brought up near the rainforests close to Mullumbimby.

'I'm soooooo fancy,' I warbled, quickly followed by a click of the fingers, slightly out of time with the rhythm.

'Trash the hotel. Let's get drunk at the mini-bar!' sang my eleven-year-old.

Before Iggy can rap another word, I quickly hit the power button to stop the music.

'Mum, what did you do that for?'

'Those words aren't good . . .'

'But why? I like Iggy's long blonde hair and she knows Nicki Minaj.'

'I'm not a fan of singing about the mini-bar,' I replied, already regretting this conversation.

'What's a mini-bar?' asked Giselle from the back seat.

'It's something that is far too expensive and that you would never open anyway.'

'What does that mean?'

'Let's put Taylor Swift back on.'

Thankfully, I no longer had to hover at the bottom of hot, silver slippery dips or splintery ladders at the play-ground to keep my daughters safe. But that constant vigilance to protect my girls from physical harm had now been replaced by the trickier job of keeping them safe from the pressures of growing up too fast! And I understood that it's not unusual to want to grow up quickly, having been in a hurry when I was a teenager.

Also, it's not surprising that Allegra has inherited my love of fashion and make-up. Since she was tiny, she has played in my messy Aladdin's Cave of a ward-robe and has seen me combine all manner of feathery, sparkly and cat-patterned outfits. Recently, though, I explained that she couldn't wear my gold-studded ankle boots (which she fits into already) with her denim miniskirt and Rolling Stones T-shirt.

'It's way too grown-up, Allegra!'

'It's in my blood though, Mummy. I'm a fashionista!'

'I love that you're a fashionista but you're not wearing that! Take off the boots and put on your sneakers with it instead!'

'You just don't understand!' said Allegra, stomping off still wearing my boots, into her bedroom.

It's alarming the flashbacks I'm now having to almost identical conversations that I had with my own mother when I was younger. When I was just a few years older than my daughter is now, I used to leave the house in jeans and a T-shirt, and hide my 'proper' outfit in a clean garbage bag in our bin. Ducking behind our fence, I'd ditch the jeans for super-short electric-blue bike shorts and a mesh midriff top.

#CRAPHOUSEWIFE

When I was a teenager I wasted far too much time focusing on what was 'missing' instead of marvelling at my natural beauty and strength. Now I have many wishes for my daughters, one of them being that they're aware of their pure loveliness. Looking back at old Kodak photos of my girlfriends and me lounging in the midday sun on Camp Cove Beach in Sydney, what I see are exquisite young women all with their own individual beauty. We wore impossibly high-cut black one-pieces with thick gold bracelets and cuffs that we wore up to our elbows. Sadly, all my sixteen-year-old eyes could see then were the stretch marks that I used to count in the bathroom mirror.

During my mid-twenties I lived with a doctor who was training to be a plastic surgeon. While he was studying the vast medical tomes for his degree, I became engrossed in some of his textbooks too. I was particularly taken with the before and after pictures of breast implants. I had always been flat as a pancake and I had briefly flirted with the idea of getting a boob job. Teardrop-shaped implants were new on the market and supposedly gave you a more 'natural' look. Apparently the look that surgeons were going for was no longer Pamela Anderson's buxom breasts but more Elle Macpherson–style cleavages. Thank goodness my implants remained a daydream. I would have looked absurd with big boobs as my body would have looked out of proportion and comical, like a Chupa Chups lollipop. Still, I wasted too much time counting my stretch marks in the mirror.

Early on in my courtship with Peter, I often wore wondrously padded bras under white angora polo-necked jumpers. He still teases me about my 'false advertising' during those days of getting to know one other. When my bra, which was a marvel of engineering, unclipped from the front, all it revealed was my AAA-cup breasts. Once I became pregnant, I managed to let go of my body hang-ups. Those stretch marks, old and new, became the songlines of my body. During both of my pregnancies, I was able to briefly experience the joy of having bigger breasts and I found myself frequently transfixed by my cleavage! Much of those nine months was spent looking down at my D cup that was frequently flowing over. I'd never had that line between my boobs before and previously to get that effect I had to wrap my arms around my body and give myself a hug!

#CRAPHOUSEWIFE

Okay, so I'd ruled out long ago having plastic surgery on my body but was I now being a hypocrite for deciding to have some cosmetic treatment on my face? Grappling with my conscience meant I kept my botox plans to myself. Instead of researching medical textbooks, this time I found myself studying friends' and strangers' faces as well as googling every conceivable article on injectables. Eventually, I decided to talk to my dermatologist about the treatment. He had been treating me for adult acne and after each appointment I ended up grilling him about botox too. On top of my own research, I had been sneaking the brochures from his waiting room about cosmetic procedures into my handbag, to study them more closely at home.

The first time I had botox done was just before Allegra's first birthday. My dermatologist calmly explained the procedure to me and then got me to sit very still while he carefully drew spots of a medical-grade permanent marker onto my face as a guide for where he would inject the botox. Despite the numbing cream he had rubbed onto my face, it still hurt. But I wasn't going to complain as I knew the pain was totally self-inflicted so I just closed my eyes, took deep breaths and tried my best to relax. But the strong smell of the antiseptic, alcohol-impregnated towelettes the nurse used to rub the black marks off my face quickly brought me back to my senses.

Looking in the small, oval-shaped mirror that I'd been handed, all I noticed were little red pinpricks on my forehead, around my eyes and between my eyebrows where I'd been injected. The doctor explained that I would probably start to notice a difference in a week or two. Apparently everyone responded at different rates to the treatment. The redness disappeared quickly and over the next week I noticed my brow looked tighter and those fine lines around my eyes didn't look so deep.

However, I was still able to raise my eyebrows high as I helped my blonde-headed daughter blow out her one pink candle on her Barbie-doll birthday cake. That first year of your child's life is all about survival, and this party was also a milestone for Peter and me. Licking the sweet buttercream icing off my slice of cake, my heart was full as I watched my husband snuggle our firstborn in his arms. She was dressed in a white tulle fairy dress and giggled as her father paraded her through the party.

'Isn't she the most beautiful girl you have ever seen?' he said as he gently stroked her damp baby curls around her forehead.

Earlier in the morning, I'd clipped back part of Allegra's longer fringe with a small, glittery butterfly clip. While I secured it gently into her fine, blonde hair, I spoke softly into her ear.

'Oh my baby girl, we have come such a long way, my darling. Thank you for being patient with your mummy.'

#CRAPHOUSEWIFE

Mentally I was back, after surviving post-natal depression with the help of medication, my psychiatrist and family, but physically I was still exhausted. I was tired and anyone with small people in their lives understands the exhaustion that seeps into every pore of your being thanks to the culmination of not enough sleep night after night. Sleep became my obsession and the ultimate aphrodisiac. I found myself frequently engineering games that involved me lying down on the floor while my energised little daughter played around me.

'Mummy is just going to rest her eyes and pretend to be a sleeping giant. She cannot wake up until the princess has stacked all of her blocks on top of Mummy's stomach! No, I don't mean whack them into my eyes! Princesses have to be gentle as well as strong . . .'

Another good game was playing 'operations'. A game that we played a lot as Allegra got older. It was especially handy when I was pregnant for the second time. Now it was harder to get rest so I was desperate for any excuse to be horizontal. The 'rules' of this game meant Mummy had to lie down with her eyes closed because of the 'strong medicine' she had been given by the doctor/daughter.

'Mummy has to stay asleep for a long time, like the princess from *Sleeping Beauty*,' I said.

'I'm not a princess, I'm Allegra!'

'That's okay because you're a doctor and doctors have to work very hard to make their patients better. And it's going to take a long, long time to make Mummy better, so I'm going keep my eyes shut just in case.'

Not surprisingly, Allegra would get bored with this game pretty quickly. However, I would try to stretch it out, which meant sometimes being covered in permanent marker, bandaids or lipstick. Any amount of short-term pain or stain was worth the chance of closing my eyes for just a few more minutes. Apart from being physically exhausted, I was also over seeing my weary face in the mirror, and not just because it was covered with red

felt-tipped pens. So I tried to ignore my skin-deep con-
cerns and made a point of not spending too long peering
into the bathroom mirror. I felt guilty wasting time on
my wrinkles, as I kept remembering Mum's refrain to my
sisters and me when we were growing up.

'No Prince Charming is going to come along and rescue
you. It's up to you to make something of yourselves. And
that's not going to happen by looking in that mirror! Go
and do your homework. And once that's done, please
clean the kitty litter. I don't want to have to leave it in
your bedroom again, Jessica.'

Now as a 'grown-up', cleaning the kitty litter (and
cleaning in general) still isn't one of my strong points.
One of my friends still gives me birthday gifts of scented
candles each year to combat the ammonia smell of the
litter! My nose was still immune all these years later but
my eyes had become sharper at noticing the wrinkles
on my face. However, part of my 37-year-old self was
embarrassed about 'wasting' time over my looks as I
remembered those lectures from Mum. So I didn't tell
anyone what I was getting done. I was too embarrassed
to tell my husband as he also didn't have much time for
people who spent too long looking in the mirror.

#CRAPHOUSEWIFE

For the next few months I was doing some fill-in news presenting on Channel Seven. I'm sure the make-up artists who pencilled in my eyebrows and carefully applied my liquid eyeliner each morning could tell the difference. Those beauty professionals would have noticed my smoother face even though they were tactful enough not to mention it. These miracle men and women kept much more 'shameful' secrets. They regularly clipped in the fake hair of female presenters and artfully blow-dried the hair plugs that hid the balding scalps of many male television types. Many of them also saw the plastic surgery scars hidden in hairlines and behind the ears of some of the presenters who sat in their make-up chairs every day.

One person I couldn't hide my refreshed appearance from was my eagle-eyed mother. She was the first to quietly comment to me, joking that she would like to come along to the next appointment. And I was relieved she didn't give me a version of her old lecture. My sisters also noticed my slightly smoother appearance. Not surprisingly, my husband didn't notice the difference but the game was up when he beat me to the letterbox one afternoon.

'Pussycat, what is this receipt from the dermatologist?'

'What receipt?' I said, trying to buy myself some thinking time.

'The receipt that says $500 for botox treatment!'

'It was for botox . . .' I replied, knowing that there was no getting out of this.

'But that is such a waste of money, and so vain and stupid! Why?'

'Well, I wanted to get it done. And I like the way it looks.'

'You look beautiful to me. You don't need it.'

'Thanks, my darling. I do it because I want to.'

Now Peter just rolls his eyes when I tell him I'm due for another appointment with my dermatologist. And I've come to realise that there is no point hiding it from anyone else. Honesty has always been important to me and the older I get, the less I worry about what 'everyone else thinks'. Although we all know what matters most is on the inside, I know that I feel stronger and tougher if I feel good on the outside too. And I don't believe I'm erasing the experiences from my face as it's all still deep inside of me. My heartaches, my joys and my dark times. Just look at me, talk to me—those gloriously sad, bad and mad times are etched into my being. I'll always carry those experiences in my heart and in the way I live my life.

Of course some of you may think, *Oh, she's so shallow*, or *How absurd to talk about cosmetic surgery.* It probably is— but it's a choice I've made. And my brand of feminism is all about supporting women and the different choices they make, even if it's not the choice you might make for yourself. Who are we kidding if we simply pretend we just wake up looking a certain way? My doctor is cautious and conservative, which is good as I don't want to look like some of my favourite characters in *The Real Housewives of New York*. However, I'd be happy to look like Erika Jayne, otherwise known as 'The Pretty Mess', from the Beverly Hills franchise of the show. She is very open about her cosmetic procedures. My fantasy has been to join her 'glam squad' for a week in Los Angeles.

During my five-minute interview with her on *Studio 10*, I managed to borrow her diamond-encrusted Cartier panther knuckleduster, which sat ever so snugly on my finger. Who knew that panthers had green sapphires for eyes?

'People underestimate you. You're a successful pop star and you're a really smart businesswoman. That's what I really love about you,' I gushed, not being at my objective journalist best during this segment.

'Thanks very much, that's very kind of you . . .' replied Erika.

'May I have the ring now?' I pleaded.

'No, you may not!'

Later on camera, Erika invited me to be a part of her show in Beverly Hills. Well, I'm still waiting by my phone for her to call! But look out, Hollywood—I'm already hoarding my frequent flyer points. However, my husband has told me that he'll divorce me if I even consider joining the Sydney version of the show.

#CRAPHOUSEWIFE

Like Erika, it's refreshing to hear other high-profile women owning their appearance. And that's what leapt out at me in some recent interviews with these Hollywood stars. Actor Charlize Theron has revealed that she credits her fresh face to 'tons of botox. And vodka'. I wanted to high-five the *House of Cards* star Robin Wright, who said the 'secret' to her skin is botox.

'You bet. Everybody effing does it. It's just the tiniest sprinkle of botox twice a year. I think most women do 10 units but that freezes the face and you can't move it. This is just 1 unit, and it's just sprinkled here and there to take the edge off. Perhaps it's not wise to put that in a magazine? But I ain't hiding anything.'

How about we all stop hiding it! And in the interests of full disclosure, I also get botox in my armpits. Not because my armpits are saggy and wrinkly but as a treatment to stop excessive sweating! Now I don't mean damp under-arms, I mean heavy sweating that marks your clothes and is impossible to hide. For me, this problem became especially noticeable when I began reading the news on Channel Ten over 25 years ago. It was the nineties and the age of the pastel power suit. Despite keeping my arms firmly by my sides, the heavy perspiration marks would still show through my suits every evening while I read the news bulletin. Adrenaline combined with nerves conspired to reveal how much I was struggling to keep it all together beneath the heavy make-up and strong lights on the news set.

For some time, I looked like a startled gazelle reading the news. My father used to leave a message with the station switchboard every evening during the news bulletin. He would put on a variety of accents ranging from Indian, Italian to Irish to disguise his voice, praising 'that lovely new girl reading the news. She's doing such a good job!' However, his 'accents' were wasted each night because he would end up leaving his real name with the receptionist at Network Ten. It became a regular joke with her. Each night, after I walked out of the studio, she would tell me, 'Your dad has been ringing again!'

As well as the moral support from Dad, my mother gave me some more practical advice. She suggested using sanitary pads in my jackets to absorb the sweat! Each evening before the news, I would jam these super-sized pads into the armpits of my blazers. It wasn't successful and instead I just looked like I had huge, fat armpits. During the commercial breaks I would rush into the make-up room and use a hair dryer to disguise the wet marks. It was embarrassing and I tried every deodorant on the market. Nothing really worked, so to deal with my shame I ended up choosing darker suits and avoided silky, light fabrics that would show up the sweat. This was something that happened during all my jobs on television. And there were a lot of jobs.

It wasn't until I started having botox on my face that my doctor explained that botox could also be used as a treatment for excessive sweating. Although you need a lot more units of the product in your armpits, the cost was worth it. Not only did I save on clothing and dry-cleaning bills, there was no longer the added stress of worrying if the sweat was showing through my clothes on television. No longer did the long-suffering wardrobe staff have to wait on stand-by with the hairdryer, ready to blow-dry my armpits in the commercial breaks.

These wardrobe warriors are the unsung heroes of the media. They have to wrangle egos, dispense the best outfits to hide any number of flaws and enhance your good points, as well as be 'on call' therapists. One tolerant wardrobe girl I knew had the unenviable task of cutting perfectly positioned holes into a presenter's Spanx so she could use the toilet without having to get undressed! This person also insisted on having her 'body control garments' laundered at work instead of taking them home to wash. Television is so glamorous, isn't it?

#CRAPHOUSEWIFE

Beauty is only skin-deep. Some of the most physically flawless people I've met have also been some of the most unhappy and self-absorbed individuals, held hostage by their looks. By comparison, the most beautiful people I know are self-confident, compassionate and funny. One of my hopes for my daughters is that they love who they are, and realise what beautiful souls they are growing into. Like my mum, I want to steer them away from spending too long in front of the mirror. Hopefully, I'm showing them that the most beautiful part of someone is their heart and the ability to seek out joy in the big, wide world. However, I'm a long way from being perfect, having recently buckled under the demands of my United Nations-style peace-negotiator eldest daughter who is now the proud owner of two Kylie Jenner lip kits.

HONEY AND SOY CHICKEN WINGS

Mum used to make chicken wings for my sisters and me when we were little, and I remember the four of us would sit around our kitchen table licking the sticky marinade off our fingers. Now it's my turn to make chicken wings for my daughters and Mum, when she stays with us once a week.

Ingredients
1 kg chicken wings (you could also use drumsticks)
½ cup honey
½ cup soy sauce
2 tbsp of vegetable oil
1 packet microwave rice (you can choose from brown, basmati, jasmine or long grain—this is the best and only way to cook rice)

Method
Preheat oven to 200 °C. Marinate the chicken wings in the soy sauce and vegetable oil. (I put mine in a foil barbecue tray as it saves on washing up!) Roast for half an hour, turning the wings regularly.

Then tip the honey over the wings and cook for 15 more minutes. This stops the wings from turning into charcoal! Neesy gave me this tip, and ever since I've added the honey at the end it has saved batches of wings.

Moments before the chicken is ready, cook your microwave rice. (I'm always looking for shortcuts and this is one of my favourites!)

Serve the wings on a bed of rice.

Success rate

Three out of four family members love this! My husband made it clear from the start of our relationship that he won't eat chicken wings or chicken drumsticks as, 'There's not enough meat on them, Pussycat!'

4

Friends

My friends are my estate.

EMILY DICKINSON

'Can I ask you a favour?' I asked, leaning across the narrow table in the coffee shop.

'Sure, what do you need?' replied my friend Pip, craning her neck to hear my unusually soft voice.

'I need you to check my hair.'

'It looks great, I love the colour . . .'

'No, I need you to *check* my hair,' I paused. 'For nits!'

'Absolutely,' replied Pip, as we both started scratching our heads.

'Not here, but can you do it in my car?' I asked.

Without missing a beat, Pip paid for my coffee and together we walked back to the nearby supermarket carpark. For half an hour we sat in the back seat of my car while my dear friend carefully looked through each strand of my hair. And that, for me, is the definition of a true friend.

The power of female friendship is a force to behold. So I wasn't surprised by the results of a recent Harvard study that found having female friends is scientifically proven to improve your health. The study found that the effects on the health of women without female friends can be as toxic as cancer! Having my girlfriends—my own tribe of warrior women—has been a lifeline that has kept me sane. This tribe of women has shrunk in size the older I get through a combination of factors: for example, my conscious decision to surround myself with good people and let go of those toxic friends who suck all my energy. But what I'm less proud of is that my circle has contracted because of my own sloppiness around maintaining some healthy friendships. I'll start with the relationships that I regret letting slip through my fingers.

There's my dark-haired, green-eyed pal Georgia who endured endless playground sessions with me and our kids. Every Thursday afternoon we would spread out our stained picnic rug in the park, order takeaway pizza and hot chips and compare notes. The pair of us would debate about: whether cargo pants could ever be stylish (no!), federal politics, the best way to get poo off wooden floorboards, and whether we'd ever get paid work again. We would get so absorbed in these discussions that sometimes we missed preventing our tiny children from ducking behind a tree to go to the toilet.

Georgia had kept me sane during those mind-numbing afternoons of swings and sandpits. She was an early ally, someone who I could talk honestly with about the boring bits of having little children. We had first met in prenatal classes and thanks to Georgia's organisational skills we started catching up again when I had the confidence to leave the house with Allegra. It was a huge feat getting out the front door with a little baby, and sleep deprivation combined with the Herculean task of packing all the equipment I needed for one small soul were often enough to make me want to stay at home. I'm glad that Georgia made me get out of the house to meet up each week with our babies.

We also had our second children at the same time, so again we were stuck together in the trenches of tedium and utter exhaustion at the same period. Our shared experience helped me to survive as often the highlight of my week was getting together with our small children in the park. I'd chase the dirty grey pigeons off our picnic rug to stop them from eating our prized chips, while Georgia would try to stop our eldest kids from walking straight over the pizza boxes, squashing their dinner, in their rush to get to a rare spare swing they had spotted at the other end of the playground.

The swings were my favourite part of the park. And that's a big call because playgrounds do my head in. No, I didn't enjoy the endless pushing or the way my heart would stop when I saw any child walk too close to the front of the swing while it was in mid-air. But what I loved about the swings was that I could strap Allegra into it, preventing her from wandering off around the park. This moment of containment meant a delay in any brawls or 'negotiations' between my daughter and other kids over buckets and spades in the grotty sandpit.

'Let's count to 50, Allegra. How about 50 more pushes on the swing?' I suggested, pushing Allegra on the swing.

I was perfectly balanced; able to push her with one hand while I cradled my other hand around her baby sister Giselle, who was strapped onto the front of my chest in her Baby Bjorn sling.

Since I was busy with this balancing act, I was able to ignore the little boy dressed in a blue Octonauts T-shirt who was patiently waiting for his turn. I'd successfully avoided eye contact with his mother, whose laser-beam look said: 'For god's sake, get your daughter off the swing. It's my son's turn *now*.'

Reluctantly, I unstrapped Allegra and she scampered across the park to join Georgia's son on the pirate ship.

The pair of us laughed when we spotted our kids on top of the pirate ship, the pair of them spinning the plastic steering wheel wildly next to another little girl. Georgia was by my side as we managed to convince the kids to share their captain's duties with the other girl. She was my wing woman and her like-mindedness helped me to shrug off the glare of other mothers that I could often sense in the playground. Her stories, solidarity and healthy, hard-to-find snacks helped glue us together during these years in the wilderness with our small children. However, circumstances, including her moving interstate and my inability to return text messages, have conspired to keep us apart for too long.

#CRAPHOUSEWIFE

Another treasured friend who had kept me afloat when I was sinking in quicksand was Suz. At the time my career was in the toilet, I was suffocating under baskets of dirty washing and my brain was a mush of pureed apples and failed controlled-crying routines. Suz got me—she understood me—and her friendship was a connection to an earlier life but also to a future. Although I was struggling, I knew I'd be okay because although we lived in different cities and we didn't see enough of each other, I knew my girlfriend was out there. I could call her,

I didn't have to pretend life was sparkling and I knew she would listen to me. And not just listen but really hear me.

But getting a spare, uninterrupted millisecond to chat on the phone was an impossible luxury. My little girls had a honing device that meant they could ferret me out the minute I even looked at my mobile. I remember hiding in the pantry cupboard or in my bedroom with the phone trying to talk to my girlfriend. Once I resorted to throwing fistfuls of rainbow-coloured Smarties through the tiny opening of my wardrobe door to get a few more moments on the phone (a handy technique that I have used a lot over the years). We made up for those half-finished stories when we would see each other, maybe twice a year. The time lapse between seeing each other didn't matter; those years would fall away and the pair of us filled in the missing gaps with laughter, tears and gifts of diamantes and leopard print. It was an easy friend-ship—easy because of the lack of pretence between us. She knew the warts-and-all me, and I didn't need to make an impression. And I'm sorry that I've let this beautiful girl slip out of my life.

#CRAPHOUSEWIFE

What about those friendships tinged with envy and jeal-ousy? I admit I haven't always been an angel in this department as I've been guilty of feeling that gentle stab in the heart when a friend's career takes off at the same time that mine has been floundering. Of course, I now realise it's more about me and my insecurity about some of my professional failings. It's been revealing for me to recognise my habit of criticising people that I had perceived as doing 'better than me'. Now I've discovered that the happier I am, the more I'm able to celebrate other people's success rather than having that destructive voice inside me, saying: 'Why isn't that me? It's not fair . . .'

Unfortunately, I've been guilty of letting both good friends and toxic friends leave my life in the same way. I now realise that this is not very brave of me and I have a habit of walking away from difficult conversations. This has meant some friendships have ended not through my pure laziness but because they were destructive and energy-sapping for me and my spirit. Friendships shouldn't be hard work; sure, relationships need to be nurtured but once it becomes exhausting you need to find an exit clause. However, I've always been hopeless at 'breaking up' and have used the very same traits and techniques to end friendships that I had raged about former boyfriends using against me all those years ago. I start by not returning phone calls—calling people back has never been a strength of mine. But I know that this behaviour sends out mixed messages, as I'll also forget to call good friends back.

Let's have a look at those friends you need to remove from your life. Firstly, there are those high-maintenance type of friends—the ones that call on you for every 'crisis' . . . and everything in their lives is a crisis! I've had my share of one-sided friendships where it's all about the other person. Listen, I can debrief relationship breakdowns, the merits of one type of baby wipe over the other, the best padded bra, and why Brandi is the best housewife in *The Real Housewives* franchise for weeks. But the conversation can't always be heading in the one direction. More and more I'm trying to take note of the mantra I teach my daughters: that 'friends are people who make you feel better about yourself'.

Pip, my nit-checking friend, has introduced me to the notion of Zone One friends. A clever concept, which I've told her she must copyright! Basically, your friends in this zone are the ones who are good for your soul, understand your flaws and when you spend time with them, they leave you feeling energised. They are your people! You can put other friends into Zone Two, Zone Three etc in descending order of importance. Sure, these people are still your friends, colleagues or pals, but you work out where they fit into your life and only give them the appropriate time and energy that the relationship deserves.

Some of these 'outer zone' friendships may be based more on sharing the same experiences at the same pivotal points in your life. These might be friends you went to university with, or met on a dance floor in a foreign city, were single, had kids of the same age, or are school mums. Occasionally, people who really are Zone Five friends may behave like they deserve to be in your Zone One. I'm gradually getting better at realising where people fit into my life and I'm learning not to exhaust myself to keep everyone else happy at my own expense.

My friend the psychic medium and teacher John Edward has a wonderful term for people who zap your energy and leave you feeling inadequate. He calls them 'negative ninjas'; people who suck your life force and make you question everything from your choice of lipstick to how you discipline your kids, and your choice of life partner. Our time is far too precious to waste on souls who don't have our best interests at heart.

#CRAPHOUSEWIFE

Recently, I listened to a marvellous interview with Australian artist Davida Allen. She spoke about the 'magic fairies' who bring people into your life when you need them. I've never stopped believing in fairies and this notion of sparkly souls bringing good people into your orbit resonates with the part of me that is always looking for the magic in life. Never, ever lose sight of the joie de vivre that friends can bring to your world. I'm trying more and more to treat these treasured relationships with love and care.

I'm convinced the 'magic fairies' brought Denise Drysdale into my life. Even though I'm not sure what Neesy would make of this theory of mine. The pair of us met through work when Neesy joined the panel on *Studio 10*. We've only known each other for a couple of years but it's such an unexpected delight when you meet someone who truly gets you and makes you laugh. Neesy brings out my even sillier side, which I'm embracing more and more the older I get. Unlike me, she has no problems with difficult conversations and has no problems letting people know exactly where they stand. Neesy has tried to encourage me to be a little more like that but I'm not there yet as confrontation has never been my style.

'You could always poison them,' says Neesy. 'And if that fails, there's always electrocution!'

Not only does she make me laugh as she tries to help me with life's bigger issues, as I've mentioned earlier, she introduced me to a life-changing ingredient—the panko crumb—for my cooking! She also comes over to clean out my fridge, sort out my pantry and tries to organise my life! It's really an uphill, lifelong battle as no one has yet been able to make me neat and tidy.

There's an extra lightness to Peter's voice when he knows that Neesy is around since she'll cook enough food to last our family for weeks. She makes the best roast chicken in the history of the world (she learnt the fine art of basting in her family's chicken shop), serving it up alongside crunchy roast spuds, cauliflower in white sauce and gravy. Apart from her caring and culinary skills, Neesy is often the voice of reason when it comes to my daughters.

'You let those girls walk all over you!' says Neesy.

She's the only person who I would let say this to me.

'You need to say "no" more often to them. But I know you won't!' she laughs, while I nod my head, laughing along with her.

#CRAPHOUSEWIFE

The pair of us have been doing a regular podcast together, called *One Fat Lady & One Thin Lady*. The title is a variation of the *Two Fat Ladies* cooking show. Surprisingly, our podcast name caused concern with some of our listeners, who told me that I'm not all that skinny and Neesy isn't fat! Yes, that's a valid argument but it's meant to be a joke and we love poking fun at ourselves. For me, laughter is a very important ingredient in any good friendship.

We haven't got any budget for marketing our podcast, so Neesy came up with the idea to dress up as a 'podcast', take to the streets, and film people trying to guess what we were! My job was to dress as the 'pod', so I leapt at the chance to wear a bright-green pea-in-a-pod suit. You know how much I adore any type of costume. It was remarkably easy to order a convincing pod costume online but it was harder to find any 'cast' costumes for Neesy. Plenty of hospital-grade bandage supplies came up in my google search but nothing looked right (and it was all too expensive, especially since Neesy loves a bargain). Eventually, I bought a pile of discount bandages from Chemist Warehouse, which I wrapped around Neesy's head and arms before we leapt onto unsuspecting shoppers in the city.

'What am I?' I asked a charming older gentleman, who instead of stating the obvious—that we were lunatics—said, 'You look lovely!'

'Oh, thank you,' I said.

'What is this, though? What do you think?' said Neesy, adjusting my pea suit to get rid of the wrinkles.

'P, ppppoood,' Neesy and I said in unison.

'I'm a pod.'

'What am I?' asked Neesy.

'You've been in an accident!' said the gentleman, sounding concerned.

'Noooo, we're a pod-cast!' we both laughed.

'I've never heard a woman snort before!' he said. 'It's very nice!'

Later that night, I decided to surprise Peter by wearing my pea-in-a-pod suit to bed. Neesy had encouraged me to do it too and we both thought it would be hilarious. While I was waiting for Peter, I took some selfies and sent them to Neesy to keep my spirits up while I got hotter and hotter, hiding under the doona.

At last I heard him walking up the stairs.

'Pussycat, what is this clutter everywhere?' he asked. 'I bet other people don't have stuff in their house like this.' Even though Christina, our cleaner, still came once a week, it was a challenge to keep the house spotless between her visits. There were piles of paper, coloured pencils, books, lip glosses, cushions, empty bowls and pineapple plastic cups scattered around upstairs.

It took every ounce of my self-control to remain quiet under the doona. He then came into our bedroom and flicked on the light as I leapt out from under the covers.

'Surprise!' I shouted.

There was dead silence as Peter looked at me for a moment.

'Are you alright?' he asked.

This was not the reaction I was hoping for.

'Don't you think it's funny?' I said, storming out of the bedroom in my costume, furious that he didn't find it even slightly amusing to find a life-sized pea in a pod in bed. I was so cross, I wouldn't talk to him for the rest of the evening.

#CRAPHOUSEWIFE

Although I had always fantasised about having a coterie of girlfriends *Sex in the City* style, I realised that was not real life. The idea of lingering over drinks and talking about heartbreak, heartache and preferred sexual positions with my nearest and dearest has always remained pure fantasy. Why? At heart, I'm an introvert and much better at friendships one at a time and one on one. This means I have a select group of friends who bring a lot of happiness, wisdom and fun into my life.

The other precious souls in my Zone One include my darling 'Donatella', who is styling himself, his life and an extraordinary career in Los Angeles. We don't see each other enough but when we do, it's like we've never been apart. Woffy, who is my movie buddy, 'acting coach' and one of the most loyal and beautiful people that I'm lucky enough to know, is also a friend for life. My yogi guru and wardrobe mistress, Annebelle, who cast a spell with two pink candles while I went through IVF, is always twinkling in my orbit. And I'm blessed enough to also have had this type of relationship with my tight group of girlfriends from high school. We're all scattered across the globe but when we catch up, it doesn't matter how long it has been as we all click straight back into that special shorthand way of relating to those who know you best of all.

I'm not a perfect friend. I'm slack at returning phone calls and emails, and have a track record of cancelling at the last minute. My excuse of being 'busy' is not good enough—who isn't busy? Busy with our kids, careers, ageing parents and that never-ending to-do list. But now that I've left my television job I'm choosing to make more time for those Zone One friends. And that makes me happy as I can't let this handful of special women and one man slip through my fingers. But I'm not quite there yet, so please remember that just because you don't hear from me in a while, it doesn't mean I don't love you. I am trying to be more reliable.

Even my husband has been known to call my number eight, nine, ten times a day to get me to ring him back. When I worked at Channel Ten, if he couldn't track me down on my phone he used to call one of the producers I worked with so he could talk to me! I'm one of those people who often has her phone on silent and then I forget to switch it back on. Now that I've left work, he'll call our local coffee shop to find me as that's where I'll often do my writing and 'work'.

Friendships do change as we grow and I've learnt that that's okay. The key is to know which ones to let go of but, more importantly, to take the time to nurture those special stars in your constellation, even if you're at different stages in your life journeys. To those glorious people who have been by my side when I've needed you most, please don't give up on me. Even though I've gone missing in action at times, remember that I will always love you.

TUNA NIÇOISE SALAD

This is a recipe from the wonderful Justine Schofield. It's a super easy but tasty salad with enough ingredients to fill up a hungry husband! It's from her book *Dinner with Justine*. Although Nigella Lawson's first impression of my rendition of this dish was a slightly surprised one due to the addition of rice into a salad Niçoise, it's an absolute winner for our family. It's a great summertime lunch or dinner. It's also a good one to impress your guests with. And I love it because there is minimal room for disaster as there is no cooking required for this dish (other than putting the rice in the microwave).

Ingredients

2 × 185 g cans of tinned tuna, drained

2 cups of long-grain rice (I use a large bag of trusty microwave rice)

250 g cherry tomatoes, cut in half

½ red capsicum, cut into strips

1 continental cucumber, halved and cut into cubes

50 g small black pitted olives

4 hard-boiled eggs, cut in half

10 basil leaves, torn

Salad dressing

2 tsp Dijon mustard
½ garlic clove, finely chopped (I crush mine)
1½ tbsp red-wine vinegar
120 ml extra-virgin olive oil
salt flakes and freshly ground black pepper

Method

Flake the tuna into a large bowl. Add the cooked rice and the remaining ingredients.

For the dressing, place the mustard, garlic and vinegar in a small bowl and whisk to combine. Next slowly whisk in the oil, then season with salt and pepper to taste.

Pour the dressing over the salad, making sure it coats all the ingredients.

Success rate

Two out of four family members absolutely love this. However, the girls spend far too long picking out everything they don't like from the salad. It's simpler to just give them tuna and rice and then make this salad for Peter and myself.

5

Courage

It is never too late to be what
you might have been.

GEORGE ELIOT

Carefully, I tiptoed around the coils of brown rope holding
up the gold brocade curtains. It was pitch-black and my
eyes were slowly adjusting to the darkness. No one else
was around but I didn't have much time before the stage
manager found me and told me to go back to my dressing-
room. Earlier that day, the cast had been given a briefing
on the 'dos and don'ts' of the theatre. So I knew I wasn't
meant to be wandering around this backstage area on my
own. But this was too good an opportunity to ignore since
usually I was in the audience, sitting in the red antique
velvet seats gazing up at the performers.

Tiny specks of dust danced across the stage, catching the light reflecting off the ornate baroque walls of the theatre. The smell of popcorn still lingered, making my tummy grumble especially loudly because I had been too nervous to eat much that day. Tears began forming in my eyes, it was so beautiful looking out onto the dress circle. Each day I had worried about why I was doing this. I had asked myself, 'Would people laugh at me but not in a good way?' 'Would I forget my lines?' 'Would I muck up my dance steps?' 'Would my daughters suffer since I hadn't spent much time with them during this mad month?' 'Had I wasted my father's time, since he'd been staying with us to babysit the girls while I worked late into the night?'

However, when I stood grounded to the stage, all of those noisy words of self-doubt disappeared. This glorious, golden moment of stillness and wonder and the butter-flies in my stomach were worth all the weeks of rehearsal, fear and lack of sleep.

'Jess, is that you up there?' asked Bonnie, the director and producer of the show.

She had appeared out of the dark, at the sound desk at the back of the theatre. There were just a few hours until showtime and she wanted to finalise the lighting cues.

'Oh, I'm sorry, Bonnie. It's just so beautiful up here,' I said.

'My darling, you just enjoy it. Thank you for saying yes . . .'

At last I was relieved that I'd said yes to accepting the role of the empress in the pantomime *Aladdin*. Bonnie Lythgoe, the British actor, dancer and theatre producer and director had brought her love of pantomime to Australia because she was passionate about introducing a whole new generation of children to the theatre. This was the second time she'd directed and produced a pantomime in Sydney and she had patiently combined a cast of professional performers alongside people like me! My emperor was my friend and long-time television and radio host Jonathan Coleman. The pair of us would settle our nerves during dress rehearsals with Lindt chocolate and inane chatter.

Jono took to writing his lines with black texta on the palm of his hand. The problem was that the words would smudge as his palms sweated with nerves and the pair of us ended up repeating our lines over and over again to one another. During rehearsals, while we waited in the wings preparing to walk onto the stage, I'd remind Jono of what scene we were about to perform. Then in our downtime, I'd disappear to the bathroom for a nervous poo! Thank goodness Bonnie had given me my own dressing-room.

On our first night I strode out onto the stage in my floor-length red gown, wearing a dazzling paste crown on my head, and roared out to the audience. Those nerves soon disappeared to be replaced by adrenaline and then relief when I heard them laughing at my first joke. It was such a blast pretending to be a conniving, domineering woman for a few hours a night. When my daughters first saw me on the stage they couldn't believe that this shouting, scary woman was their mummy. My mother had suggested that I apply some of my character's no-nonsense approach to my real life. We both knew that would never work because if I ever tried to shout at home, my girls simply laughed at me. And their dad wasn't far behind me in not being taken seriously by our daughters when he got cross with them. At heart, we're both softies.

#CRAPHOUSEWIFE

Although I wasn't getting better at 'discipline', I had been getting better and braver at saying yes to unexpected career opportunities. What had helped me take these leaps had been my role as a panellist on *Studio Ten*, which had helped me to find my voice again and to stand up and speak out about the many social and political issues that we debated on the program. Every day I wore my heart on my sleeve when we argued about an issue and I could never be half-hearted about anything we discussed, regardless of the subject matter.

Too much of my early years had been wasted on worrying about what other people thought, and now I was
determined to keep putting myself out there. For me, being
brave was about remaining true to myself and showing
up despite still feeling afraid of the consequences. But it's
never straightforward, as sometimes you imagine it would
be simpler to lead a small, quiet life. Being brave means
ignoring that bowel-churning fear, that never totally disap-
pears, and instead listening to your heart. Often it's easier
to be logical and rational but it's far more rewarding and
meaningful to tap into our instinct and to listen carefully
to what it is guiding you to do.

Recently though, I was almost sabotaged by that fear
before a presentation that I was doing for Facebook in
Asia. I was going to talk at a conference in Singapore
in front of hundreds of their staff from the region and
Sheryl Sandberg would also be attending it. The night
before my speech I had a chance to walk onto the stage
and run through my slides with the organisers. During the
rehearsal I realised the goose bumps on my skin weren't
just from the arctic air-conditioning that was blasting
through the giant function room. I was nervous and I
also realised that I was terrified by the enormity of the
opportunity that was now sitting heavily on my shoulders.
There was that all-too-familiar voice popping back into my
head: 'What do you know?' 'Who are you to be talking

to these incredible women?' 'You're not enough' 'You can't do this.' I tried to push those fears away but I kept second-guessing myself once I left the stage.

While I looked out from my hotel room high over the Singapore skyline, I still couldn't quieten those negative thoughts. Once I drew my eyes away from the pink lights and back into my spotless room, I needed to again go calmly through my speech for the next day. Scattered across my giant king-sized bed were my notes, a variation of the presentation that I had given hundreds of times over the years. It was part of my story: a story about the impact mental illness can have on your life, the importance of asking for help and about how embracing imperfection can help you lead a bolder and braver life.

But I had started to second-guess myself. How relevant was my story to women from Korea, Japan and India? Tomorrow I would be sharing the stage with a woman who'd escaped from North Korea and devoted her life to empowering women and children. Who was I to tell the women in the audience, many who had overcome far greater obstacles than me, my story? Despite having this luxury king-sized bed to myself, I didn't sleep well that night as I kept rewriting my speech in my mind, over and over again.

Early the next morning my mobile rang, as my daughters wanted to wish me luck before they headed off to school. Peter got on the line to say goodbye and he could hear the strain in my voice. Before we said our farewells he reassured me that he'd call back soon.

When I answered the phone an hour later, I heard Peter's loud, clear voice on the other end of the phone.

'Pussycat, I've got the girls to school, I've fed the cats, and Christina has just texted me to say she can't come today. Anyway, tell me, are you ready for today?'

'Sort of . . .' I said.

'What does that mean?'

'I didn't really have a good sleep. I was thinking about my speech all night. I'm going to change it,' I answered tentatively.

'But what do you mean you're changing it? It's your story, Jessica. Just tell them your story!'

'What if it's not enough?'

'It is. You've got this. Talk to them like I've heard you give this talk so many times.'

After we'd said goodbye I allowed my husband's words to sink in, relieved that he'd come to my rescue, as he'd done so many other times. And I knew deep down what I needed to do. Our stories are what connect us—we may not remember facts or figures but what we do remember is how someone's story makes us feel. All any of us wants is to feel understood.

Just a few hours after my husband's pep-talk phone call, I danced onto the stage to the lyrics of Taylor Swift's 'Shake it Off'. I asked all the women in the audience to join me in shaking their wrists as well, and told them to shake off the pressure to be perfect. As I shook my wrists again and again and wiggled my bottom, slightly out of time to the music, I shook off that pressure I had put onto myself. Although my fear was still lingering in the background, I put my heart on the line and drew on my courage to tell my story. There were laughter, smiles, tears and some nodding of heads as I gave my speech. Afterwards, many women came up and shared their stories with me too. It didn't matter where we came from or what our cultural norms were, we all had something to share with each other on that particular day.

Later that evening, I headed to the bar perched on top of my hotel and I ordered my first Singapore Sling. The balcony was crammed with fellow tourists also trying to capture their picture-perfect moment but there was a minimum US$200 spend if you wanted a window seat, so I made do with a stool squashed at the end of the busy bar. When no one was looking, I managed to drag my stainless-steel stool right over to the edge of the Perspex balcony. Slowly sipping my slushy-like flavoured cock-tail, all I could now hear was that positive voice inside me, cheering me for getting through the day. There was nothing more I could have done. Peter was right, it was enough. I was enough.

At other times in my life, I've also given it my all but it hasn't always worked! An experience that comes to mind was my disastrous year co-hosting the *Today* show for the Nine Network. I've written in detail in my memoir *Is This My Beautiful Life?* about this period, so I'm not going to revisit the politics, the cruelty and the vileness of some individuals. Here is the abridged version: I was employed to do a job but thanks to forces within the Nine Network combined with sections of the print media, I was sacked from my job while I was on maternity leave. I'm still at a loss to understand what my crime had been to have been treated in such an appalling way.

On only my second day as co-host, I remember hiding in my dressing-room before the show to read newspaper headlines likening my appearance to a velociraptor. Remember those skinny, mean-looking dinosaurs that were the villains in *Jurassic Park*? The columnist said I had 'razor-sharp, short blonde hair', and described my chemistry with co-host Karl Stefanovic as 'thrusting a hand towards her co-host like an over-friendly raptor'. The article concluded with the line: 'It had been three hours but it felt like three years.' Those words hurt even though I had expected to be criticised when I signed up for the job. Not everybody was going to like me and I'd wasted too many years seeking their approval. Who were these people? Well, they were some of my peers in the media, members of the public and media bosses.

Constructive criticism wasn't a problem because despite reading the news for ten years, I knew I had to fine-tune my broadcasting skills that I needed for interviewing and ad-libbing for three hours of live television each morning. But what wasn't helpful during this period of intense learning was the nasty criticism that dominated much of the media coverage about me. My intelligence, appearance, weight and loud laughter were frequently called into question. One commentator summed me up this way: 'Rowe has the long limbs and angular face of a model; she is childless and loud.' No one knew at the time that Peter and I were going through IVF and were desperate to have a family. When the criticism reached a crescendo, I was in the early stages of pregnancy with my Allegra. She was my sweet secret and she kept me going because her very existence taught me about fighting for survival. She blossomed from just 'one good egg' during our third IVF procedure, into a three-day-old cell and then into a healthy, somersaulting baby that was pushing at the sides of my tummy, eager to enter the world.

But I'm not going to devote any more time trying to make sense of that year. I refuse to be a victim of circumstance; instead, I'm a glorious, glittery survivor. All of us have challenges that can make or break us and now, more than ever, I'm a believer in sticking those cracked pieces back together to rise into something far more beautiful. Initially, it looks like failure and for a long time, I felt like a failure. But we don't learn about our strength, our resilience and our power when life is easy. Author Brené Brown sums it up perfectly: 'There is no greater threat to the critics, cynics and fearmongers than a woman who is willing to fall because she has learnt how to rise.'

Brené's words inspire me to keep showing up and to keep striving through the tough, sometimes soul-destroying times in our lives. My counsellor first introduced me to Brené's work a number of years ago when I was trying to make sense of the destruction of my career. If you're looking for meaningful motivation, I encourage you to also check out her TED talks and books.

#CRAPHOUSEWIFE

For me, life is about being thankful for the forces of love and strength that I received from good people who helped me to rise back up. I learnt about the power of love, the love and ferocious loyalty of my husband who was willing to burn down his own career in defence of mine. We had both been working at the same network and his moral code couldn't reconcile how an organisation where he'd spent most of his professional life would deliberately seek to destroy his wife. For once in our partnership, I had become the more sensible one and convinced him that we still needed to pay the mortgage so it was counterproductive for us to both be unemployed. Besides, I wouldn't allow him to throw away his boyhood dream of being a news broadcaster.

I had experienced firsthand the destructiveness of words in print, but I also drew courage and strength from the written words of decent men and women. These journalists, politicians, feminists, athletes and entertainers whom I'd admired from afar leapt to my defence with letters, emails and phone calls of support. And I also experienced the kindness of strangers who also wrote to me, emailed me and stopped me in the street for a hug and some words of solidarity.

And most importantly, it was the ferocious, fierce love that I had for my unborn baby that helped me to rise up too. My baby girl was still safe inside of me, stretching her mermaid limbs in translucent amniotic fluid. And I needed her to know how much you had to fight for what mattered in your life. Her father and I had fought hard to make sure she would have her place in the world and my first lesson for her, even though I was unaware of it at the time, was that you had to keep 'showing up'. She learnt via my lifeblood that to live a large, brave life, you needed to take risks. Even if it might on the surface appear to end badly.

#CRAPHOUSEWIFE

Another example of being professionally bold (or possibly stupid) was my decision to do *Dancing with the Stars* for Channel Seven. My confidence had been shattered after I had been sacked from the *Today* show but I was still desperate to have another shot at a job in the media, having invested much of my life into building my journalism career. Ignoring the sage advice of my husband who accurately reminded me that I couldn't dance, I somehow managed to convince myself that this offer to be on a dancing show would be my only chance of a comeback on television.

'Ladies and gentlemen, please welcome to the floor Jessica Rowe and her partner Serghei Bolgarschii.'

Serghei grabbed my hand as we walked in darkness to our places on the dance floor. Wearing a cat suit and black sequinned pussycat ears, I sat on the bottom of the stairs and carefully arranged my feather boa tail behind me to avoid any tripping hazards once we started our foxtrot dance routine to the song 'Love Cats' by The Cure. The piano began to play and I stretched out my black-gloved hand to Serghei.

This routine was the highlight of my short stint on the show and I still have the feathered catsuit costume squashed into my daughter's wardrobe. One day I'll wear it again! During rehearsals for the show, I had revelled in the opportunity to get out of the house and apply my discipline to learning complicated dance routines. However, all of my hard work became unstuck when it was time to perform in the live shows since I would get extreme stage fright whenever we had to dance in front of anyone else. Slightly problematic when that was the premise of the program! Each Sunday evening, before we had to dance live in front of a studio audience and television cameras, I stood clutching Serghei's hand, feeling sick to my stomach. What on earth was I doing here? I tried to calm myself by drawing on the advice of showbiz queen Patti Newton, my dressing-room buddy who told me, 'You just have to let go'. It's funny how closely her advice mirrored what I did on the Facebook stage a decade later in Singapore when I told the audience to 'Let go of those expectations and shake it off like Taylor Swift.'

Another time when I put every ounce of my energy in going for an opportunity was when I auditioned for *Play School* a few years after doing the dancing show. Now I had two little girls; Allegra was five years old and Giselle was three. I had been doing occasional fill-in news presenting on *Weekend Sunrise* but it wasn't enough to restore my confidence as I was still struggling to find regular television work. What were my talents? Hey, I play dress-ups and sing with my girls, so I thought it would be a cinch to work as a presenter on *Play School*, the long-running children's show on the ABC. Conveniently, I didn't focus on the fact that I really couldn't sing!

'Red and yellow and pink and green, purple and orange and bluuuue. I can sing a raaaaainbow, sing a raaaaainbow . . .'

'Stop it, I don't like it,' Allegra complained.

'How about this one? The dinosaurs were dancing round the prehistoric swamp. They shook their heads, swished their tails and . . .'

'No more singing, Mummy,' my three-year-old Giselle said bluntly.

With my daughters pretending to be mermaids wearing their green Princess Ariel tails in the bath, I rehearsed my songs over and over again to them. I knew I had a captive audience because those tails meant they couldn't get out of the bath in a hurry. And, boy, I needed all the practice I could get for my *Play School* audition.

Just a week later I found myself having an out-of-body experience in one of the vast ABC television studios at Ultimo in Sydney. Despite my valiant efforts, I warbled on through 'Sing a Rainbow', a song with far too many key changes for an amateur like me. That part of the audition finally ended as I attempted to trace the shape of a rainbow in a jumble of hand movements. Then after I'd energetically leapt through the story of the dinosaur stomping through the forest, with Groucho Marx eyebrow movements and spectacular sound effects, I was swiftly shown the door by the director.

One of my personality traits apart from persistence is stubbornness and I wasn't ready to say goodbye to Big Ted and Little Ted just yet. Realising I needed professional help, I enlisted the expertise of *Play School* royalty, my friend Jay Laga'aia, who listened patiently while I read him some kids stories. Jay told me to lose the newsreader precision and perform like I was simply talking to my daughters. Next, he played some songs on his piano while he heard me 'sing'. The sounds coming out of my mouth weren't even close to the notes but Jay was still encouraging and gave me the number of a fabulous singing teacher.

My desire to crack the nursery-rhyme code led to the beginning of a special friendship with my singing teacher

Margi. It wasn't about hitting the right notes—my renditions of 'Little Peter Rabbit' and 'Sing a Rainbow' were still all over the place but I discovered such simple delight in that weekly singing lesson. It was my time, my bubble, just for me. There was no one there to judge, snigger or criticise me, so I let the notes, rhymes and vibrations caress me. Singing scales, flubbering my lips and blowing fart sounds while making a cat's bum face brought me such pleasure!

Finally, I got a second crack at *Play School*. Jay went over all the moves I needed, coaching me through the steps known as the grapevine. Margi got me as close to the right notes as I was ever going to get and this time there was no out-of-body experience as I shook my head and wiggled my tail for the director. Even my dinosaur drawing wasn't too bad. I finished the audition knowing there was nothing more I could have done. The phone call came a few weeks later but unfortunately I still wasn't good enough. I sulked for a few days but had no regrets.

#CRAPHOUSEWIFE

Not only had those singing lessons helped me to get in tune with myself again, they were an entree into the enchanting world of theatre and the talented, passionate souls who tread the boards. Through my singing teacher

I met some more of her students and friends, who took me under their costumed wings to perform as the narrator (no singing required) in the musical *Side by Side by Sondheim*.

'Don't go, Mummy. You can't leave!' Allegra said, her surprisingly strong hands grabbing around my waist and stopping me from getting out the door.

'It won't be long—it's only four sleeps and you'll have so much fun with Grandyfrog (her grandfather). You love it when he looks after you. He lets you drink Coke and stay up and watch all the Harry Potter movies,' I said, wondering why Allegra never gave her father a hard time when he had to travel for work.

We were about to tour the Sondheim show well off Broadway, playing theatres in a couple of country towns in New South Wales and Victoria.

'No one else's mummy goes away. You always go away.'

'Don't be so ridiculous. I never go away! I'll be back soon. And I'll bring you a present.'

'Another cat?'

'We'll see!'

Each night of the tour, at the time I would usually be dealing with dinner, bath and bed for my girls, I revelled in putting on false eyelashes and slipping into a black sequinned cocktail frock. When I walked on stage accompanied by the pitch-perfect tone of two baby grand pianos and grasping my hand-held mic, I knew my butterfly wings were shimmering and that, for now, it was my time.

My music theatre career might have only lasted a few weeks, but those steps out of my comfort zone paved the way for the more confident strides I took onto the State Theatre's stage as the domineering empress in the *Aladdin* pantomime. And that's what I want my darling girls to realise, that you need to keep taking those steps to lead a brave life. There is not one of my fabulous failures that I regret. My dream for my daughters is that they too will leap for the stars. Sure, they'll have those moments of fear, tears of frustration and anger at the unfairness of it all at times, but I still want them to go for it. I want them to remember the words of the poet Erin Hanson who says, 'What happens if I fall? Oh, but my darling, what if you fly?' And what I love about Hanson's words is the sense of optimism that underlies taking such a leap of faith.

So my darling girls, always remember that if you don't fly the first time, I will always be there to catch you.

CHICKEN AND CASHEW NUT STIR-FRY

This stir-fry recipe is from *MasterChef* star Adam Liaw. I have a track record for making soggy stir-fries; however, I've made this recipe successfully. Not surprisingly, I don't have a wok so I cooked it in my trusty frypan. And I also made it without onions and garlic as these ingredients weren't in our cupboard *and* I knew the girls wouldn't eat them!

Ingredients

500 g chicken thigh fillets (I bought them already cut into cubes at the supermarket)

1 tbsp soy sauce

1 tbsp Shaoxing wine

2 tsp cornflour

¼ cup vegetable oil

3 slices ginger (I left this out as I know my girls won't eat it)

5 cloves garlic, peeled and roughly chopped

1 small brown onion, peeled and cut into 3 cm chunks

½ red capsicum, cut into 3 cm chunks

½ yellow capsicum, cut into 3 cm chunks

½ green capsicum, cut into 3 cm chunks

½ cup of unsalted roasted cashew nuts

SAUCE

2 tbsp oyster sauce

1 tbsp soy sauce

1 tbsp Shaoxing wine

1 tbsp white vinegar

1 tsp sugar

¼ cup of chicken stock (or water)

Method

Combine sauce ingredients in a bowl and set aside to marinate. (I left out the Shaoxing wine as I only had rosé in the fridge!)

In another bowl combine the chicken with 1 tablespoon of soy sauce and 1 teaspoon of the cornflour (this was a revelation—it made the chicken SO tasty!) Mix well to coat the chicken.

Heat your wok/frypan over medium to high heat adding 2 tablespoons of oil. Add ginger and garlic (if your kids will eat it) and toss for about 30 seconds until the garlic is browned. Add the chicken and cook until browned (this took me a few minutes, I also cooked the chicken in a couple of batches). Once the chicken cubes are cooked, remove from the pan and set aside.

Put remaining 1 tablespoon of oil into your wok/pan and add capsicum (you could put onion in at this stage but I left it out, because the girls won't eat onion either) and cook until the capsicum starts to soften.

Return the chicken to the wok, add the sauce, stir and bring to a simmer.

Finally, combine the remaining 1 teaspoon of cornflour with 2 tablespoons of cold water and drizzle this mix slowly into the wok/pan and stir until it thickens slightly. Toss through the cashews and serve.

Serve the stir-fry with rice (again using that microwave rice that comes in a bag from the supermarket).

Success rate

Two out of four family members loved this! Peter couldn't believe that I made it! Allegra had a few mouthfuls of stir-fry but both she and Giselle ended up eating the plain chicken without the capsicum and cashews.

6

Sex

No woman gets an orgasm from shining
the kitchen floor.

BETTY FRIEDAN

My husband is terribly nervous about this chapter.

'You're not going to write about sex, are you? Don't write about our sex life . . . You are NOT going to. Come on, Pussycat. Enough is enough!'

'No, Petee, I won't . . .'

'Promise? Because I've heard Kyle Sandilands say he does it Peter Overton-style in the kitchen!' said Peter, explaining that just that morning he'd heard Kyle mention it on his morning radio program, the *Kyle & Jackie O* show.

I laugh, reminding him that he must have been talking about that one sentence I wrote in my last book about us having sex on our kitchen benchtop!

'And you had the chance to read my edited manuscript before it was sent to the printer. But remember you didn't want to read it *and* I told you if you weren't going to, then you couldn't complain about what was or wasn't in the book,' I replied, aware that my strident-sounding voice was also because I hadn't meant to embarrass my dear husband.

#CRAPHOUSEWIFE

Here is the disclaimer about this chapter: it's **not** about the sex life of Peter and me. So, from the title of the Salt-N-Pepa song, one of my dance favourites and a song whose nineties beat and catchy, cheesy lyrics would get me attempting to hip hop in my younger days: let's talk about sex, let's talk about you and me (not my husband and me, but generic you and me!). I want to talk about sex and whether any one of my vintage is having much sex anymore.

Rationally, I tell myself that sex isn't about how many times you 'do it' a week and I know that knee-buckling feeling between your legs can ebb and flow. Generally, women need more time to get into 'the mood'. And yes, I know that's a generalisation but I'm basing this observation on myself and the chats I've had with my girl-friends. My desire for sex has diminished simply because I'm too tired! For me to get into the right headspace, I need time—a lot of time—and not the worry that our bedroom door will be shoved opened by insistent, oblivious little people.

What is enough sex? And how much sex 'should' we be having? I've never been a fan of the word 'should' because it's loaded with guilt and expectation. Don't we put ourselves through enough of that nonsense? Plenty of inexact science has been done around the actual amount of sex that couples are having each week. According to the Sexual Wellbeing Survey sponsored by Durex, six out of ten Aussie couples are having sex once a week. Let's remember that this condom company has an interest in couples having a lot of sex! Another survey claims married couples are having sex, on average, six times a month. Are you having more or less? Normal? Abnormal? Okay, after you've done the mental calculations perhaps the self-doubt starts to creep in, like it does for me. And suddenly you're thinking your sex life is on the skids.

Not so, according to sexologist Dr Nikki Goldstein. She says there is no right or wrong amount of sex for couples. She says that couples who don't have sex can still have a good relationship. Ummm, really? However, Nikki says this only works if you *both* don't want to have sex. But is there a way to ignite your naughty side when you feel out of practice and would rather eat chocolate in bed while reading a Swedish crime thriller? What is the sure-fire way to find your missing mojo?

Dr Goldstein is a believer that having a 'quickie' is one way of getting those sex hormones firing again. She says sometimes you need to 'use it or you lose it'. But it doesn't have to be 'wham, bam, thank you ma'am' because despite what some blokes say, sex doesn't have to be about penetration. She says that sexy notes, text messages and compliments are all ways you can get those endorphins moving again. Why not take a moment to get into the right headspace and remember the things that turned you on about your partner? For me, there is nothing better than watching Peter dressed in black tie talking to a room full of people. I love just to sit back and watch him . . . Hold on, this isn't about us!

#CRAPHOUSEWIFE

Why not ignore the domestic drudgery, the rushed good-byes in the morning and tune in to what you find sexy about your partner? Betty Friedan wrote about the myth of women's domestic fulfilment in her book *The Feminine Mystique*, which became a rallying cry for the feminist movement of the 1960s. And a part of me imagines that she would also have been a proud craphousewife, as she urged women to ditch their vacuum cleaners and embrace their many talents. Women have great fantasy lives, so take a moment to clear out all the stuff in your head and focus on what makes you blush and unravel in the best possible way. Good sex is about what works for you and not some glorified, false image we see on Netflix, in movies and pornography. The only porno I've seen, I remember the bloke wore a beret and nothing else. And it was the most unsexy thing I've ever seen! Most pornography is made by men, for men, and some of those bizarre positions have been designed not for our anatomy but solely for the camera. You won't reach nirvana that way and all you will get is a crook neck and an emergency appointment at the physio. Book some time for the two of you, consider organising a regular 'date night' where you endeavour not to talk about your kids for the entire time. Rediscover the part of yourself that melted at the right touch of your lover. But if you can't do that, at least get a childproof lock on your bedroom door.

When Allegra was just a toddler, I remember her sweet little face would be pressed up against the shower screen while I tried to have a moment's peace to think about the day ahead. It wasn't long before she worked out how to push open the Perspex shower door, so she would also get herself wet while I quickly rinsed the two-in-one shampoo and conditioner out of my hair. Showers would last 30 seconds and it was little wonder that the hairs on my legs and armpits needed their own postcodes. I was far from feeling desirable.

#CRAPHOUSEWIFE

Although my heart would physically ache if my daughter was too far away from me, it was hard to ignore my growing irritation over my diminishing amount of personal space. And that irritation would grow in direct proportion to how little sleep I was getting each night. The ultimate aphrodisiac for me had become sleep and I'd turned into one of those people who, when I finally got beneath the covers, would say out loud, 'I *love* bed!'

I hadn't expected that staying at home with my daughter would be a struggle; the loving part wasn't hard but nothing had prepared me for the permanent fog of exhaustion that I stumbled through every day. Sure, there were those moments of bliss but it seemed like I had lived a lifetime in one day: changing endless nappies, wiping down benches, doing incessant loads of washing and building up stacks of blocks only to have them knocked down moments later. My darling daughter pulled on my legs, hid under my skirt and constantly demanded my attention.

Now I laugh with my mum when she reminds me that I had been exactly the same when I was a little girl. She would take my sisters and me to Centennial Park to 'play' as we didn't have much of a backyard. Once we got to the park, settling down near a duck pond, we'd sit all over Mum like a litter of puppies rolling around the picnic rug. The three of us were oblivious to our mother's desire for some personal space.

#CRAPHOUSEWIFE

Since becoming a mum, I was craving my own physical space too. Once I'd managed to get Allegra into bed, I definitely wasn't up for anyone else's demands for my attention. Desperate to have my body to myself, I would hold my breath if my husband rolled over, stretching his arm around my waist. Lying still, I would have everything crossed so that his hand would stay exactly where it was.

'Can't you just hold me?' I'd ask.

'Oh, but I know I can get you in the mood,' Peter would say.

'Nothing will get me in the mood. Just give me a cuddle, I'm too tired . . . I love you.'

'But what about me?'

'Go and take a cold shower . . .'

My tolerant husband would sigh, roll back over and turn on the radio. As he struggled to tune it in to a talkback station, the baby monitor playing havoc with the reception, I would be already asleep and snoring, very loudly. My heavy sleep would remain undisturbed until I heard the chirpy sounds of my daughter through the monitor, ready to start her day, despite the sun still hours away from waking up.

Life hadn't always been like this, and I wondered what had happened to that careless, carefree young woman I had once been. How were other mums coping with the changes in their bodies and the never-ending demands on their emotional energy? Was that mother with her toddler in the stroller I saw each morning at the cafe too exhausted for sex too? Or was it just me?

#CRAPHOUSEWIFE

The words of Cat Stevens' song 'Wild World' thumped out through my boom box and I turned it up super loud, dancing around the small sunroom that was my bedroom in the unit I lived in with my mum and two sisters. Twirling around wearing the short, black, ruffled skirt that I had bought from Sportsgirl along with the red polka-dotted midriff top that mum had sewn for me on her Bernina sewing machine. There was something about these earworm lyrics that got me fantasising about a jet-setting, glamorous life.

Each weekend I worked as a check-out 'chick' at our local Woolworths and I spent my money on clothes and Malibu. My girlfriends and I would mix that foul coconut-smelling alcohol with giant cups of Coke that we'd buy from the movies before heading out every Friday and Saturday night.

Make-up was still relatively new for me and I'd taken to disguising my acne with black kohl pencil. I'd read in *Dolly* magazine that turning pimples into beauty spots was the best way to camouflage blemishes. That might have worked for one or two pimples but it wasn't ideal for the severe acne that I had on my cheeks. However, I've always been an optimist and convinced myself I'd done an okay job at hiding them. Besides, the bright-red glossy lipstick I was wearing was enough to draw attention away from my black spots.

The Cat Stevens song that I had played on repeat in my small bedroom became an anthem of sorts for me, as I dreamt of escaping what I thought was a narrow, small life. I was almost eighteen, no longer a virgin and like all teenagers naively thought that I knew everything. The big, wide wonderful world was waiting for me and I wanted to face it with my eyes wide open. So I fled, just down the road, to a waitressing job in a fancy cafe where its outdoor tables were the most prized position as it was still a novelty to eat outdoors in Sydney. We hadn't yet caught up with the rest of the world but this pocket of the eastern suburbs of Sydney was determined to be like Paris or Rome.

The designer-clad ladies who lunched had no idea we were making their cappuccinos with one giant heaped teaspoon of Nescafé and a blast of boiling water. The only genuine part of the cappuccino was the frothy milk, as the milk steamer was the only reason the owners had purchased the big, shiny, silver coffee machine. It was far cheaper for them to stick with instant and the pretence of good European coffee. Imagine how revolting those short blacks must have tasted with three heaped teaspoons of instant coffee! But they were popular to order as I think some of the customers thought it made them look sophisticated, even if they couldn't drink them.

Unfortunately, I didn't last long as a waitress because I muddled up too many coffee orders and dropped too many Caesar salads into the laps of women wearing their new Trent Nathan blazers and dark-blue denim jeans. Pretty soon I was banished to the takeaway counter in the cafe and it was here that I met the ticket out of my boring life. He was over 6 feet tall, had a deep, raspy voice and ordered a mixed salad and a banana smoothie. And he also happened to be twenty years older than me.

Let's call him Mr 37. I was under the misapprehension that dating him would make me sophisticated and sexy.

He was handsome, he owned a nightclub, a plane and a yacht but he did have a saggy bottom! Not surprisingly, my mum banned me from seeing him, claiming he was a drug dealer and a sleaze (he wasn't a dealer and the hardest drug I ever indulged in was Midori and lemonade, having moved on from Malibu). Of course, I raged against my mum, claiming that I was in love and she didn't understand me. Then I did what all good teenagers do, ignored her demands and kept seeing my cradle snatcher in secret. By then I had become good at subterfuge, organising to stay over at girlfriends' houses for the weekend, when I was really meeting my older man in his nightclub and dancing the night away to Bryan Ferry.

My foolproof plan came undone when Mum discovered a bunch of photos. All G-rated—this was long before the era of selfies and sex tapes—but they did show me and Mr 37 riding mountain bikes and bushwalking (I hate bushwalking) on a couple of weekend getaways. She was furious that I had deceived her but was even more worried that the light plane he was flying would fall out of the sky. Mum had realised she couldn't compete with my 'massive self-will' so she stood aside, very unhappily, while I continued my inappropriate love affair.

Surprisingly, my dad and stepmother weren't as outwardly concerned. They seemed to take the approach that it was better the devil that you know. A couple of times they came to dinner with us at the nightclub, I drank Midori and lemonade, they stuck with wine, and we talked about scuba diving and parachuting. I was acting like an adult even though I still went home to sleep in my single bed in the sunroom above the busy main road with the streetlight blazing through my narrow matchstick blinds.

Although it sounds terrifying to a parent (and I'm terrified, thinking about my own daughters) it was all rather vanilla. Usually, I was home in bed by midnight and up early the next day to hit the gym with my boyfriend. He was a health nut, so if we weren't training together we were bike riding, water skiing or sailing. The sex was standard, although I did manage to get him out of his comfort zone! The stairs of the nightclub, inside his Porsche, below the deck of his yacht, and the back seat of the plane while it stayed on autopilot. Okay, it might sound raunchy but he never found my G spot and I had already become an expert at making what I thought were the right sounds. Deep down I realised there had to be something more.

And there was, as it was time to focus on my dream of becoming a journalist and start my communications degree at Mitchell College in Bathurst, in western New South Wales. Not surprisingly, my simple student life in a country town wasn't a turn on for Mr 37. He did fly there a couple of times but I kept hearing from my city friends that in my absence he was entertaining international models from Sweden on his yacht in Sydney Harbour. Soon after, our affair ended and I was heartbroken. But when you're young your heart mends faster than you realise and I become even busier starting my brand-new life.

#CRAPHOUSEWIFE

Midway through my journalism studies, I took a year off to travel and model in Europe. It was the first time I'd been overseas and I couldn't wait to get those stamps in my passport. Now I use the word 'model' loosely to describe my job, as that part of my international modelling career was limited to sporting and camping catalogues in Germany. An agency based in Munich had signed me up from Australia because it thought I had potential in the lucrative world of mail order catalogues and television commercials.

The highlight of my less-than-brilliant modelling career was starring in an ad for washing powder in which I wore white underpants and a singlet while filling up the front-loading washing machine. It was so unremarkable that my part got cut from the ad before it even made it to television. It's little wonder that I still fail at loading the washing machine all these years later!

I had been hoping to also try my luck at modelling in Japan after my year in Germany was wrapping up, but I also knew I needed to finish my university degree. I had a carefree and wild year living in Europe and it would have been even longer if university had given me permission to defer my journalism studies again. There wasn't any rush to leave my exciting life. I'd met new friends and all of us had wanderlust and we were having the time of our lives. No one knew me, so I could be whoever I wanted: desirable, confident and indestructible. Once the sun went down, evenings became a blur of tequila shots, music and nightclubs. It was easy to make friends in this hothouse of hormones and youthfulness.

This beautiful abandonment when you're young was typified by a holiday in the Greek Islands that I shared with a girlfriend, halfway through my overseas adventure. Each morning I woke up in my small clifftop hotel room, bright-eyed and clear-headed despite my nocturnal naughtiness. My eyes would squint as I opened the blue shutters of my bedroom to gaze onto the Aegean Sea.

Later in the day, wearing just black bikini bottoms, I would roast my body under the cloud-free sky, oblivious to the strength of the Mediterranean sun. Lying on my blue, striped beach chair rented for a handful of drachma a day, my bare skin was protected from the white pebbles of the beach and also gave my friend and me a lazy position from which to check out the handsome blokes. That summer we were young, untouchable and bulletproof. And that made it easy to get 'in the mood'.

#CRAPHOUSEWIFE

That island escapade was a lifetime ago. Some 27 years later, I'm far happier in my skin but I miss some of that sexy spirit from the younger me. Lusty, hot and dirty sex is something that needs time to flourish in your mind and body. And now I was struggling to transform from a crap housewife into a sex goddess once the lights were switched off. Getting in the mood and slipping out of your angel wings takes time and patience. We're great at multi-tasking but the downside of juggling so much in your mind is that it can be hard to switch off that part of the brain that's filing away parent–teacher meetings, reminders about buying white bread, finding lost library books and solving work politics. None of those mundane matters are sexy.

How would I cope if my daughters experimented like me? I would freak out just like my mum because I now realise that Mr 37 had taken advantage of my youth and vulnerability. However, I understand that I was also complicit and I knew what I was getting into. I'd been seduced by the ticket he offered me into a seemingly more glamorous and grown-up world. And I don't regret it for a moment.

Still, with some years before my daughters become young adults, I'd like to think that I would deal with a similar situation in a calm, reasonable manner. But who am I kidding? If anyone breaks their hearts, I would probably torch that individual's car. And I don't think my husband would be as 'calm' as me! But I do want my girls to have a healthy relationship with sex as they grow into strong, confident young women. My wish is that they'll have partners who make them laugh, and who love and respect them. I also want them to grow up realising pubic hair is natural and desirable and that pornography is not what making love is all about. But most of all I want them to talk to me, even if I am the world's most embarrassing mother.

WALDORF SALAD

This foolproof salad is a family favourite! My mum used to make it for my sisters and me when we lived together in our tiny unit over a busy main road. I remember thinking the salad was super fancy as it's named after the Waldorf Astoria Hotel in New York. It also reminds me of my favourite *Fawlty Towers* episode when Basil Fawlty angrily tells his fussy American guest that 'we're just out of Waldorfs!'

Ingredients
1 barbecue chook
1 big bunch of green grapes
2–3 sticks of celery
2 Granny Smith apples
a couple of good handfuls of walnuts (as many or as few as you'd like)
mayonnaise (I'm a lifelong fan of Praise—something Mum always had in the fridge)

Method
Remove all of the white meat from the barbecue chook and place in a decent-sized salad bowl.

Next, put in the green grapes. Slice up the celery into medium-sized pieces, cut up the apples and then add celery and apple to the salad bowl. Add the walnuts (I like a lot as they add a delicious crunch to the salad).

Finally, generously squeeze the mayo over the salad and give it a good stir to make sure it's all mixed through.

Season with salt and pepper. Serve with crusty bread.

Success rate

Four out of four family members loved this salad! However, I do take the celery and walnuts out for my smallest daughter. This is an ideal summer salad. And it's my favourite type of 'cooking' since all that you need to do is chop and assemble!

7

Cleaning

The opposite of a hot mess is cold, predictable and
tidy. That's not where your magic lives. Be brave
and choose the mess.

ELIZABETH GILBERT

Flick, flick, flick. I woke to the sound of my husband's
black rubber thongs flicking against our wooden floorboards in the kitchen, the sound echoing around our
quiet house. Thankfully, it wasn't loud enough to rouse
our daughters from their dream-filled sleep. I've learnt to
judge the tone of our morning by how quickly his thongs
are flicking against the floor. Oh dear, this was sounding
a little too speedy for my liking. I thought, *It's going to be
another one of those days . . .*

Since leaving morning television, my body clock has clicked straight back into its natural state of not wanting to wake up too early. Even as a small girl I was a night owl, never wanting to go to bed in case I might miss out on 'something'. Last night I read past midnight, slowly sucking on squares of dark Lindt chocolate, desperate to finish Liane Moriarty's latest book. That time, when even the stars have tucked themselves up, is my favourite hour as I relish being awake while the rest of the house sleeps heavily. The light on my Kindle is dimmed to its lowest level, so I don't disturb Peter, and I also remain motionless lying on my side, so I don't wake our elderly grey cat, Alfie. He curls his round, fuzzy-felt tummy around my feet for warmth.

But there was no gentle wake-up for either Alfie or me this morning.

'Pussycat, up! Up! Come on!' Peter shouted up the stairs.

'I'm coming . . .' I replied, while Alfie leisurely stretched his front paw over my legs and yawned.

'No you're not. Get UP!' said Peter, with an extra edge to his voice. Those flicking thongs were getting closer, as my impatient husband walked into our bedroom.

'Pussycat, Christina is coming today. There is a lot of cleaning to do!' he said.

He had a benchtop cleaner in one hand and a cup of coffee for me in the other. Believe me, I know how lucky I am to be married to this man.

#CRAPHOUSEWIFE

For some reason, my husband has always cleaned before our cleaner Christina comes for her sometimes weekly visit. She has been in our lives for a long time and first started cleaning up my life when I was a single girl with only one cat—a tortoiseshell called Audrey—for company. And boy, the two of us could make a mess. I still blush remembering my first encounters with Christina's thorough approach to her job. Opening the door to my rental unit, when I came home from reading the news on Channel Ten, I was hit by the unfamiliar scent of bleach and strong disinfectant. My unit had never been so squeaky clean and organised. My sense of wonder increased when I walked into my bedroom; my perilously high stilettos had been neatly stacked into matching pairs under the frame of my wooden double bed, and the bed itself was far too beautifully made with tightly tucked-in sheets to even consider pulling back the covers. However, when I opened the drawers at the bottom of the wardrobe, my heart sank when I realised that most of my lacy underwear was missing.

Before I'd left for the work that morning, I'd hastily chucked all of my underwear out of the dirty clothes basket back into my drawers. Why would I do that? Well, I hadn't wanted Christina throwing my 'delicates' into the washing machine. Remember, these where the days long before I even knew that comfy 'granny whacker' beige undies existed. Clearly, Christina had realised how messy I was when she first saw the state of my unit but now I feared she would also judge me as a total grot who left dirty underwear in her drawers! From that day forward, I put a sign on top of my laundry basket asking Christina to *please* not wash it. I'd tried to explain the mix-up over my smalls to her; however, I don't think she ever truly believed me. Not surprisingly, Christina has a much better relationship with Peter and the pair of them happily compare notes on cleaning products and fresh vacuum-cleaner bags.

#CRAPHOUSEWIFE

Most Tuesday mornings, Peter and I have the same conversation, with my husband arguing that it's respectful to make sure our house is spick-and-span before Christina's visit. He's far more decent than me, as I try to reason that the whole point of having Christina is to take the stress out of housework. Clearly, we have very different ideas about what 'clean' means as I've always been oblivious to the piles of mess in our home. Peter, however, can't deal as well as I can with unsightly piles of clothes, toys, newspapers, magazines, books and kitsch in the house. It's a miracle that he's put up with me so long, especially given my penchant for collecting cat figurines, cat cushions and snow domes.

We have this marvellous Harry Potter-style cupboard under the stairs, which has become a cavernous dumping ground for all manner of things. Shoes, schoolbags, recycled shopping bags, beach towels, giant cat masks, ugly prints that were presents from ex-partners and whatever else I can pile into it. This giant cupboard has become particularly handy when it comes to a quick clean before last-minute guests arrive as I'm the queen of shoving a large number of objects into a limited space in record time. This leaves me five minutes to give the toilet bowl a quick check and the bathroom sink a speedy wipe-down. (But for some reason we never have enough toilet paper, despite Peter always buying in bulk because 'It's on special'.)

'Come ON, Pussycat! If you don't get up, the girls won't get up either. Come on, I really need your help. It's 6.55 . . .'

Reluctantly, I was already out of bed and already singing songs about honey bears, baby bears and all manner of silliness to get my daughters to wake up.

'Mum, stop it . . .' said Allegra.

'Sweetie Pea, let's just get up. I didn't want to get up either but at least it will stop your Daddy from carrying on a like a pork chop,' I said, while my gangly, growing daughter rolled out of bed dragging her favourite cat, Daisy, who has been snuggled up asleep next to her.

'Honey Bear, oh Honey Bear, where are you going in your underwear . . . ?' I kept singing, as I danced into Giselle's room.

Although she pretended to be asleep, tightly shutting her eyes, I knew she was awake because of the sunny smile creeping across her face. Quickly, I lay down next to her, singing quietly into her ear as I inhaled the sweet, soft smell of her hair.

'Get dressed, it's a new daaaay,' I sang.

'Jess-ICA!' I heard Peter calling. 'It's 7.10!'

'Oh great, it's 7.10!' I replied.

My husband, who worked on radio early in his media career, has a habit of giving me time calls in the morning, under the misapprehension it will make me get ready faster.

'Come on, Baby Bear. Out of bed, so we don't have to listen to these times anymore,' I said to Giselle.

The pair of us giggled as we walked hand in hand down the stairs, both rugged up in our soft, fleecy dressing gowns. But I couldn't resist resuming my singing routine by the time we got to the kitchen bench.

'Sometimes, I get confused which paws go in my shoes, Ho-NEY Bear . . .' I sang. This was my latest song, having been introduced to it on YouTube by Giselle.

'Your mother is a lunatic, girls!' said Peter.

'I love being a lunatic and at least I'm not a pork chop, Petee,' I replied, as Giselle giggled. I've always liked an audience and it doesn't matter that it's only an audience of one.

'Mummy, stop it . . .' said Allegra.

You'd think that my daughter would have my measure by now; she knows that if someone tells me to stop doing something, I'll do the exact opposite. And I can see those same traits in her.

'I've sunshine in my heart because I'm a HONEY bear . . .' I continued, encouraged by Giselle's giggles, which were now turning into laughter.

'I used to have this running smoothly in the mornings, before you decided to stop work and start mucking things up! It's 7.20 now . . .' insisted my husband.

'Okay, we've still got plenty of time. I'm just doing the girls' morning tea,' I replied, trying to force open the drawer that has become stuck with the mismatched stacks of Tupperware containers. It's always impossible to find a matching set and I'm convinced the missing lids of the Tupperware go and have a party with all of the odd white school socks. Both of these items are always without their other half in our household.

Distracted by the newspaper on the benchtop, I started reading the front page of the *Daily Telegraph*, temporarily forgetting about Peter's time calls and organising the girls' morning tea. The headline declared that Christmas carols had been banned at primary schools.

'This is the biggest load of nonsense! Where is the evidence that schools have told kids to stop singing carols for each other? What is the point in spreading such ill-informed crap? Every year there is always a slightly different version of this story . . .'

'Pussycat, you're not on *Studio 10* anymore. Stop the rant and get ready. It's now 7.35!'

'Alright, but come on, you must see how dumb this story is. This will be all over the radio today, and we'll keep hearing how it's political correctness gone mad . . .'

'Yes, yes . . . just get dressed, Pussycat.'

#CRAPHOUSEWIFE

In the early days of being a mother, I used to worry that I was the only mum who had a messy, chaotic house. Now I've stopped wasting energy on that and have become more in tune with writer Elizabeth Gilbert's way of thinking. Her approach has helped me embrace my magical, messy

approach to living. As you know, I've always had a tendency to be untidy but since having children, this tendency
has only worsened as the clutter has intensified in our
home. When our two girls were babies I used to find
the following discarded under our king-size bed: dusty
dummies and plates of green cut-up apple that had shriv-
elled to look like wrinkled prunes, porous with mould.
Most nights the dirty dishes would pile up in the sink after
the effort of cooking dinner and getting the kids to bed
had used up most of my stamina. It's extraordinary how
severe dehydration, hunger, the need to be read another
story, have the light switched on, or have the light turned
off will suddenly strike any child who is meant to be going
to sleep. Endless treks up and down the stairs with glasses
of water meant I had no energy left to deal with any more
domestic duties. Many times Peter would come home from
work and find me asleep, lying on a pillow in my daughters' doorway supposedly to get them to go to sleep!

Our study/junk-room door had become permanently
closed with another handwritten note for Christina,
blue-tacked near the doorknob asking her not to bother
trying to clean it. The room had become a burial ground
for files, old toys, photos and boxes that still hadn't
been unpacked from when we first moved here eight
years ago. What do get moved around the house are
our laundry baskets of clean clothes. These baskets get

shifted from the laundry to the living room, before travelling to the bottom of the stairs. The piles of clothes
linger on the bottom step until everyone has run out
of underpants. At last the baskets make it to the top of
the stairs and there they remain; wobbly stacks of pink
T-shirts, a never-ending combination of patterned leg-
gings, my big, beige, underpants, and Peter's giant navy
polo shirts and exercise shorts. I have a silent challenge
with my family—would these laundry baskets ever be
totally empty? And the answer is still no.

Often, especially after visiting the immaculate homes
of friends, I'd have to remind myself of some words of
wisdom from Rosa, the South American grandmother
who helped me when the girls were tiny. She told me
that a family home was a place where you lived and loved
your family—your home was not meant to be a showroom.
And who wants to live in a showroom? Rosa also gave
our family lots of practical help too, as I needed an extra
pair of hands in the afternoons after I brought Giselle
home from the hospital. Recovering from the caesarean
meant I couldn't lift Allegra in and out of her highchair
or bath, but what I also really needed was some company
during the long afternoons. Loneliness and isolation had
crept up on me the last time, and I didn't want to feel
marooned during the chaos of dinner, bath, breastfeeds
and bedtime.

Rosa came over most afternoons. In theory this was to help with the girls, but what she was really doing was helping me to believe in myself. She reassured me that I was a wonderful mother and how love was all that mattered, and she sprinkled her love throughout our house. I would take Allegra for walks to our corner deli to have some time with her while Rosa sang Spanish lullabies to Giselle before putting her down for her afternoon sleep. When we came back the house smelt of basil, garlic and love. Allegra delighted in tasting the chunky tomato sauce that would be layered through the cannelloni, and slurping the minestrone soup off her Hello Kitty spoon.

#CRAPHOUSEWIFE

Of course I appreciate that a sense of order can help calm your mind (I've got friends who need tidiness to stay sane) but there's a huge difference between having your own self-imposed standards versus feeling judged and pressured to have the beautiful life and immaculate house because 'everyone else does'. Author and activist Glennon Doyle puts it perfectly when she says: 'Let whoever think whatever.'

Too often, we see other people's 'front of house'—basically, those carefully curated Instagram, Facebook and

Snapchat images—and compare them to our 'back of house' (real life). You see these perfect homes, interiors, holidays, relationships and children and worry that somehow you don't measure up. Oh, but you do! All of us have the same 'back of house': those fears, insecurities and negative voices. For goodness' sake, let's at least aim for a level playing field if you want to start that dangerous, slippery game of comparisons. And that's precisely why I share images from my everyday life—so you'll often see dishes in my sink and cats sitting on the benchtop but you can be guaranteed that there is always, always plenty of laughter.

#CRAPHOUSEWIFE

For me, laughter has been the antidote to dealing with the challenges of life. And as I leap closer to turning 50, I'm far more self-deprecating, willing to laugh loudly and overshare the predicaments that I find myself getting into more and more. The legendary writer Nora Ephron put it perfectly when she explained that, 'When you slip on a banana peel, people laugh at you. But when you tell people you slipped on a banana peel, it's your laugh.' And Nora's ability to write stories about her family, heartache and heartbreak has had a big influence on my own truth telling. Unfortunately, though, my eldest daughter in particular doesn't see the benefits (yet) of having a mum who doesn't take herself too seriously!

'Mum, can you not do your "whoo hoo" and clap loudly?' said Allegra.

'Why can't I whoo hoo?' I asked, hoping my eleven-year-old will hear the hurt in my voice.

'Because it's embarassing . . .' she said, while zipping up her schoolbag and putting her unicorn water bottle into the side of her backpack. She had her regional athletics carnival that day and wouldn't let me drive her there, pre-ferring to take the team bus with her friends.

How come I'm an embarassing mum? Surely I am a cool mum? Okay, I might be a bit loud sometimes but I've always just put that down to being an enthusiast.

'I just clap and yell whoo hoo because I'm proud of you.'

'It's just irritating, alright . . .'

When did I start to be irritating? If you ask my husband and some of my former work colleagues, it has been in my DNA for quite some time! But when did my little girl start growing up and pushing a part of me away?

Okay, I understand that as parents we can sometimes cramp our kids' style, and as I drove out alone to the car-nival I reminded myself about how my own mum and dad were also sources of embarrassment for me, even though I now realise that they weren't that bad! Perhaps it's just that being a parent also means being an embarrassment to your children?

Once I made it to the grandstand to sit with Allegra and the rest of her team, one of the organisers approached me.

'Jessica, would you mind presenting some of the medals to our athletes in the next lot of events? We'll make sure you have plenty of time between that and your daughter's events.'

'I'd love to, thanks for asking . . .' I replied, even though I could hear Allegra already groaning.

'Mum, you cannot go near the microphone. You cannot speak in the microphone!' she said.

'I won't speak in the microphone. They've just asked me to hand out the medals, darling.'

Later during the medal presentations, I spotted my daughter laughing with her coach as she was cheekily hiding under the metal railing so she couldn't catch my eye. Although I was tempted to pretend to grab the microphone and do some singing and tell some jokes, I managed to remain on my best behaviour.

Another place where I'm well behaved is on the sidelines of my eldest daughter's weekend sport. I've only recently been 'allowed' to come along, as Allegra prefers her dad to take her along to the soccer games.

'Mum, no clapping, no cheering, don't walk near the white lines onto the field, and don't give me a hug afterwards,' she says every Saturday morning, lacing up her soccer boots before we walk out the front door on our way to another windswept sporting field.

So far I've followed her instructions; my style of clapping is the 'fairy clap' and this involves gently tapping together only two fingers from each hand; no cheering comes out of my mouth; and I try my best to stay hidden behind the other parents. After each game I point out to Allegra how 'good' I was and explain how every other grown-up, including her father, is far noisier on the sidelines than I ever am!

#CRAPHOUSEWIFE

It's impossible to always be good; being good all the time would be terribly boring. Although fashion has always been a passion of mine, I delight in getting out of my grown-up clothes, taking off my make-up and putting on my pyjamas whenever I get home. The simple sensation of having soft fleece or flannel against my skin makes me exhale and slow down. Who knew that PJs could be so calming? Ironically, I've never worn a tracksuit out of the house but I have no such qualms in wearing my pyjamas to school pick-up in the afternoons, or to the fish and chip shop where we order our regular Friday night takeaway feast of burgers, calamari rings, chips and fish cocktails.

The first time I wore my cat PJs to school pick-up, I saw Allegra's face drop when she clambered into the back seat of the car with her sister.

'Muuum, the teacher saw! Mrs Doherty saw you in your PJs!' Allegra hissed.

'Oh, darling, that's okay. She doesn't mind.'

'Mum, she saw you when she opened up the back door of the car. Promise me you won't do it tomorrow?'

'I promise, my darling heart,' I replied, explaining that it was quicker to keep my PJs on and not waste time getting dressed in 'proper' clothes so I'd make it in time to get them from school.

'At least I still have my false eyelashes on from work!' I said, not impressing her at all. Remember at this stage, I'd been leaving home early each morning for my job on *Studio 10* and had been missing out on taking my daughters to school in the mornings.

The following afternoon, I managed to get out of my PJs and get dressed in time for school pick-up. Luckily, I found a legal parking spot around the corner from the school gate, giving me plenty of time to walk up the road to get the girls from their carline. But Allegra didn't miss a trick as she looked down at my feet.

'Mum, you're not wearing shoes!'

'Come on, at least I'm not in my PJs . . .'

'Quickly, Mum, let's go to the car,' said Allegra, pulling my arm away from the group of kids also waiting outside the school gate.

She strode out in front of Giselle and me, trying to put as much distance between me and her.

'I like my nude toes, don't you, Giselle?' I said, as the two of us laughed.

On the third day, I was determined to get it 'right'. Hurriedly, I got out of my PJs, dressed in a denim skirt and top, laced up my leopard-print brogues and managed to again get to school in plenty of time to park and pick the girls up from the gate.

'Mum, can we play in the school playground?'

'Absolutely,' I replied, my aversion to playgrounds having lessened because my daughters were now old enough to share the swings and clamber onto the jungle gym without me having to be hypervigilant for any accidents or brawls over the equipment. Standing next to the flying fox, I started chatting with one of the other mums while Allegra was patiently waiting for her turn. Giselle was sitting in the sandpit, just near where I was standing.

'Mum, you haven't got ANY underpants on!' said Giselle.

'What?!' replied Allegra, as the other mums and I started to laugh.

In my haste to leave the house, get out of my pyjamas, and make sure I was dressed for my eldest daughter, I realised that I'd forgotten to put on any undies!

'Mum, I can't believe how embarrassing you are! You are sooooo embarrassing!' said Allegra.

Each night, while I tuck up my eldest daughter under her pale-pink velvet doona, we have the same conversation:

'Mum, promise me, no pyjamas, make sure you're wearing shoes. And promise me that you'll be wearing underpants!'

'I promise,' I say. And I mean it, each and every time.

TERIYAKI SALMON

This recipe came after yet more requests from Peter to have meals with protein but without pasta! I was tempted to tell him where he could shove the protein but I was inspired to cook this teriyaki salmon after a suggestion from Tracy Bevan. (I first met Tracy through her advocacy work for the McGrath Foundation. We also regularly chat over Instagram.)

Ingredients
3 tbsp teriyaki sauce
3 tbsp soy sauce
1 tbsp white vinegar
4 salmon fillets
microwave bag of rice (the best and only way to cook rice)

Method
Preheat oven at 200 degrees Celsius. Combine all the sauce ingredients in a small bowl.

Next put salmon fillets into a mixing bowl and pour the sauce over the top. (I just did this with two of the fillets as I knew my girls would only eat plain salmon.) Cover the mixing bowl with plastic wrap and then let it marinate for 20 minutes. (I marinated mine for only 10 minutes as I got impatient!)

Next put the salmon onto a baking tray (I like to buy the foil barbecue trays as it saves on washing up) and bake for around 15 minutes. Depending on how thick the salmon is and how you like it cooked, it could take longer or shorter! So keep an eye on it. Remove the salmon from the oven and serve with rice or salad.

Success rate

Four out of four! Peter and I ate the teriyaki salmon and the girls happily ate their plain salmon with rice and a squeeze of lemon!

8

School

Great minds discuss ideas; average minds discuss
events; small minds discuss people.

ELEANOR ROOSEVELT

You never truly leave school. Even as a grown-up you find
there are groups that you gravitate towards during different stages of your life. Often the joy of embarking on
the wider world outside of the school gates is that you can
reinvent yourself and find your own posse if school wasn't
your happy place. But once your children start school,
you discover all of these groups are still there—only this
time, they are parents. And no matter how hard I fight
it, I still find myself succumbing to the pressure to fit in!

Suddenly you find yourself thrown into a mix of people
you wouldn't choose to spend much time with in your

'normal' life. The only common denominator is that you have kids of the same age. And it can take some time to sort out who 'your' people are. Although I wonder if I'll ever be wise enough to take note of Eleanor Roosevelt's wisdom since my 'small mind' does delight in discussing people. There are always the cool crowd, the diligent bunch, the sporty types, the intellectuals, the party animals, the misfits and the loners. Depending on my mood and the armour I'm wearing, I can fit into most of these categories—apart from the sporty crew. The only activewear I like to get around in is my cat unitard!

#CRAPHOUSEWIFE

My daughter's big, blue eyes were widening and looking up at me, seeking reassurance. Trying to do my biggest, beaming smile, I gazed down at my first born in her slightly too big uniform and gleaming, black school shoes. She was walking awkwardly since her small feet weren't used to the clumpy confines of heavy, lace-up shoes. The pair of us were stepping over the fallen purple jacaranda flowers that were making the uneven footpath a little slippery.

'Isn't this exciting?' I said, my sweaty, nervous hand clutching my daughter's as we walk through the school gates for her first day.

Allegra didn't say anything as she looked around at the playground, taking in the bigger kids noisily playing handball. I was close to tears but I knew I needed to be brave for my baby girl. I was tempted to scoop her up into my arms and run away from this place. My school memories threatened to swamp me, taking my focus away from the separate and undoubtedly different steps and stumbles that lay ahead for my own precious daughter.

Her father and I helped Allegra find the hook with her nametag stuck underneath it, and we gently took her giant schoolbag off her shoulders. Beneath the hook was a pigeonhole for her lunch box and Dora the Explorer water bottle. Remembering the teacher's instructions for a quick goodbye, we both hugged our darling girl, before she lined up with her new classmates.

The moment we were out of the gates, the tears that I'd been holding back started running down my cheeks.

'She'll be okay, Pussycat,' said Peter, putting his arm around my shoulder and squeezing me tightly towards him.

Soundlessly, I nodded, aware that if I said anything, I'd start sobbing. Of course, Allegra would be fine but I wanted to protect her from the bullies, the strict teachers, the friendship fights and the challenges of the classroom. But wait a moment, it had only been fifteen minutes since we'd dropped her at school. There was nothing to fix—yet! When Allegra was tiny, I was a 'helicopter parent' swooping in to help. Now I was at risk of becoming a 'lawnmower parent', ready to remove any obstacles ahead for my girl.

At the end of day one, those challenges had already begun.

'I don't think I'll go back to school tomorrow, Mummy,' said Allegra.

'Why not?' I replied, trying to keep the anxiety out of my voice.

'The teachers are bossy, sitting on the mat is boring, the bell is irritating and there is too much lining up.'

I'm tempted to respond: 'Welcome to the world and I agree wholeheartedly with all of your observations.' Instead, I decided to keep it simple.

'You have to go back tomorrow.'

'But why?'

'The government says you have to and Mummy will get into big trouble if I keep you at home.'

'Well, I think Julia Gillard is stupid,' responded my daughter.

During Allegra's first year at school, she came up with many more reasons about why she should be home-schooled! This reasoning has been adapted as she continues through the education system. And I keep explaining that homeschooling would be the worst idea as I have neither the talent nor the patience to be her teacher. And her complaints about school are valid; a lot of it is boring and even as a grown-up I still find it hard to sit quietly, especially when someone is giving me instructions. I hate being told what to do and have a perverse reaction to authority by doing the opposite of what I'm told. Is it any wonder that my eldest has also inherited some of my traits?

#CRAPHOUSEWIFE

What has changed since I was at school is that the unkindness of some children seems to start even earlier than I remember. In kindergarten, my daughter had already been introduced to the world of mean girls!

Allegra had already put a cushion next to her pillow for me. Most evenings, I lie next to her in bed while she goes off to sleep.

'I don't want to go to school tomorrow . . .'

'Oh, I know that feeling. There were times when I didn't want to go to school,' I say, stroking her blonde, thick, knotty hair.

'I don't want to go. I'm not a good learner. I'm the dumbest in the school . . .' she said softly.

'You are not, you are not, you are my bright shining star,' I replied.

'But Henrietta says I can't play with her if I can't count.'

'Well, how about playing with someone else?' I say, already furious with this Henrietta.

'Who?'

'How about Roxy or Summer?'

'But they're playing with Henrietta as well,' said Allegra. 'Promise me you'll help me to like school?'

'I promise, my darling, my Sweet Pea. I promise . . .'

'Are you crying, Mumma?' asked Giselle, who at the age of three could already pick up on the changes in my voice.

'No . . .'

'Why does your voice sound like that?'

'It's just my tired voice, darling,' I replied to Giselle, while I kept patting Allegra's hair until I heard her breathing shift—at last she was asleep.

Thankfully, the soft glow of the nightlight in the bedroom the girls shared wasn't bright enough for them to have seen my tears. I was so tempted to let loose in the playground the next day as it seemed the nasty looks I'd been making at Henrietta hadn't stopped her awful behaviour. Yes, I know this wasn't terribly grown-up of me, but this girl had been causing Allegra such heartache since school began.

I couldn't even look at Henrietta's mother at the school gate any more. She must have known that something was up since we used to chat while waiting for that loud bell to ring each afternoon. But I had been deliberately avoiding her as I'd never been good at confrontation. However, now I felt ready to face this woman as I was finding it harder and harder to keep my mouth shut. There had to be a way to sort this out because my strategy of telling Allegra to simply say, 'Stop it, I don't like it,' and then walk away wasn't working.

It took every atom of self-control to stop myself from tripping up Henrietta when I saw her the next morning in the playground. I had decided to talk with the school principal who counselled me not to approach the parents directly (which was good advice) and that they'd handle it in the classroom. Their advice for my daughter and for any child that was being bullied was to keep going with the 'Stop it, I don't like it' mantra. However, it's hard to walk away when the person keeps following you. What do you do if the child doesn't stop it? Rationally, I understood that this unpleasant little girl wouldn't be the first bully in my daughter's life. And I was determined to help Allegra develop the emotional tools to cope with tricky people but oh, how I would have loved to give her perpetrator a nasty pinch!

#CRAPHOUSEWIFE

Apart from managing pint-sized bullies, it can also be challenging getting on with the other parents. Some of these parents will become your close friends since you're like-minded souls. Other parents you'll like and happily talk to at the school gates, fete or sausage sizzle. But there are always those parents who are complete nightmares—just like their children. And it can be even more challenging when your kids start hanging out with these kids. Sometimes you just have to let these fledgling friendships run their course but at the same time keep organising other play dates with more 'suitable' children (hoping that these friendships will flourish).

What are the best ways to navigate your way through the politics of the playground? I've done a survey of some school mums that I know and here are some of the strategies we've come up with.

Only volunteer if you have the time and the inclination to help out at your child's school. Don't allow yourself to be 'guilted' into doing things, otherwise you'll become resentful. Over the years, sometimes I was able to do more or less or nothing at all, depending on my work commitments.

After leaving my television job, not only did I have more time to cause chaos at home in the mornings, but I could also volunteer at the school canteen. Heaven help the kids who had to eat my sandwiches! Thankfully the ever-patient canteen manager knew of my dodgy domestic reputation and had given me the important 'meet and greet' job. Basically, this means serving the girls their morning tea and big lunch, along with supervising the high-tech scanning system the students used to pay for their ice blocks and chips. When I spotted my youngest daughter's beaming face, as she lined up with her little friends for morning tea, my throat caught.

'Hello, darling! What would you like?' I asked.

'I love you being here, Mummy . . .' replied Giselle.

'Me too. There's nowhere I'd rather be, my Honey Bear.'

Later, when I packed the hundreds of lunch orders, I wrote special notes for Allegra and Giselle on the front of their white paper bags. I drew a giant heart in black felt-tipped pen and inside the heart wrote, 'I love you SO, SO much. Love Mummy!' I've also managed to sneak in an extra chocolate chip cookie and gingerbread man into their lunch orders. The sense of satisfaction I got from these small acts took me by surprise and I loved that I was right there, right then.

My husband also loved to help out if and when he could—he looked especially fetching in the yellow fluor-escent high-visibility vest he wore supervising the carline for morning drop-off. The only complaint from the school was that because he enjoyed a chat, it could slow down the whole process. Peter also liked to do tuckshop duty because he got the best snacks from the team who ran the canteen. Often this was just as well because he doesn't get them from me!

However, if you can't volunteer or aren't willing to put your money where your mouth is, don't complain about the efforts of those who are putting the hours into running the numerous fundraising activities. A close friend of mine, who is a banker and dynamo school volunteer, had an effective strategy for serial complainers. She suggested they set up their own committee to make sure their special ideas came to fruition. And the common response from these whingers? 'Oh, we couldn't possibly do that. We don't have time!'

Another capable friend of mine, who runs large corporations as well as the Parents and Citizens at her son's school, has struggled to always keep the entire school community satisfied. The P&C (it's also known as Parents and Friends in some states) is essentially a school-based organisation made up of volunteer parents, teachers and the school principal. It helps run the canteen and the uniform shop as well as raising money for the school. Some of the parents at my friend's school had criticised the timing of school events, complaining that it was impossible for some mothers to make it to functions scheduled straight after school drop-off. My friend then organised for the next school fundraiser to be held early in the morning. But none of these complainers bothered to turn up to their specially requested event.

And I understand how time-poor we all are, so it can be surprising to learn about many of the issues some parents waste their valuable time on. I've heard of a school where there was much ado about the Easter egg raffle. A small but bolshie group of parents wanted the annual raffle boycotted because there was 'too much chocolate at Easter' (isn't chocolate the point of Easter?). Another group decided that it wasn't fair to have a raffle, as it meant some children would miss out on 'winning' the eggs. The compromise? The classes of concerned parents had their own raffle that awarded first, second and third prizes of Easter eggs, but also gave out eggs to each and every child. Here's my disclaimer for this group of class parents: I'm guilty of being one of those parents who makes sure there's a present for every child hidden in the newspaper layers of Pass the Parcel. Once, I even stole another child's Pass the Parcel present to keep my then tiny daughter happy!

But it's not only Easter eggs that can be controversial— Mother's Day stalls and Father's Day breakfasts can also be political minefields for parents. One school wanted to cancel their Mother's Day stall, as some mums thought it was 'sexist' for mums to be running a stall! The complaint was that 'it sent the wrong message to our children that mothers had to be in charge of Mother's Day!' Some dads had volunteered to 'man' the stall but thanks to this vocal minority of mums, all the mothers missed out on getting a re-gifted soap or candle from the stall! This same school also had issues for Father's Day, as this same group thought it was 'unfair' for mothers to run the sausage sizzle because not enough fathers had volunteered to run the Mother's Day stall.

Bake sales can be another battleground for parents. One of my friends, who like me is 'cooking challenged', finds it hard to ignore the pressure of replying to all the emails from parents about upcoming cake stalls. Recently, her inbox was inundated with a flurry of messages from parents keen to show off their ability in the kitchen.

'Isabella and I will make sugar-free, nut-free, dairy-free, gluten-free honey, oat and quinoa squares.'

This email was quickly followed by: 'Joseph is going to do his savoury zucchini bread.'

But before my friend had finished reading about 10-year-old Joseph's proficiency in the kitchen, there was another ping in her inbox.

'I have a fab recipe for blueberry and lemon friands. Shall I do 16? 24? What?'

Now this bragging about baking continued with emails all day, including some from parents who wrote: 'It's unfair to have a cake sale as some children are allergic to cakes.'

But cake-making doesn't need to be a competitive sport, in much the same way that children's birthday parties don't need to be, which are becoming bigger, better, brighter than I ever recall having or seeing as a little girl.

When I was growing up, we had the occasional birthday party with fairy bread, lollies and cake but nothing like the extravaganzas that some parents organise today. Some mothers seem to forget that the party is about their child and not themselves. Or perhaps I'm sounding slightly snippy about it because I've never been a confident party hostess, for either big or little people.

Please, please don't get caught up in the party pressure. For me, the best kids' parties involve soft drinks, plenty of lollies with some wedges of watermelon to placate those parents who aren't fans of sugar! But it's easy to say ignore the pressure and then still get hijacked into doing the giant jumping castles, the face-painting mermaids and fairies and the portable popcorn and slushy machines. I've done all of that and more because I would do anything for my babies. And I want to give them everything that I missed out on when I was growing up. But what I never missed out on was love—I always knew that I was loved. And no amount of smoke, mirrors and Taylor Swift impersonators will ever replace the safety of unconditional love.

'Oh, I like your theme!' said a school mother to me, as she dropped off her girl to my daughter's birthday party.

'I beg your pardon?' I replied.

'Your theme, I really like your party theme. You've gone retro!'

'Ohhhhh, right,' I said, still confused.

Once I'd drunk some pink creaming sofa, I laughed out loud, realising that my 'theme' of soft drinks in plastic cups, Cheezels and bowls of lollies qualified as a retro party!

In my attempts to avoid hosting kids' parties, I've ended up having birthday celebrations eight months late. My eldest daughter was born in January and so over the years, many of her friends have been away when it's her birthday. Sometimes I've managed to skip having a party; however, Allegra will remind me around August that she would still like to have a celebration. For some reason, when the girls were little there was a fad of the whole class being invited to the party. Thankfully, as my daughters have gotten older, that unwritten rule has changed and their parties have gotten smaller.

Another way to avoid the birthday party pressure is bribery. Or perhaps a better way of putting it is to use incentives to persuade your child of the benefits of *not* having a party! A close friend has given her daughters the option of a big-ticket birthday present item versus having a party each year. Thankfully, over time, her children have smartly selected hermit crabs, tropical fish aquariums and cat accessories over hosting a party. Another option is hosting a party every second year. However, do whatever works best for you and your family without succumbing to the peer-group party pressure. Isn't it bizarre that even as so-called adults, we can still be swayed by our peer group?

Apart from the cost of putting on a party, there is also the cost of buying pressies for your children's classmates. My daughters have a busier social life than I do with invitations to parties or play dates most weekends. One way of managing the cost of birthday presents is to consider setting a limit at the start of the year with the other parents. A girlfriend of mine says her daughter's class have agreed on a $20 present limit. Sensible stuff. Unfortunately, I've never been good at being sensible but I'm going to suggest this to our class group soon.

Also, keep it simple when it comes to the cake. I'm always looking for shortcuts and the best types of cakes are the ones you can buy from the supermarket. But if you fancy yourself as a cake decorator, buy a plain sponge cake, cut it into any shape you like and decorate it with colourful icing, freckles, lollies or whatever your child likes. Play to your skill set rather than succumbing to the expectation to make everything from scratch. Life is far too short wasting it on cakes that will never rise properly!

BANANA AND COCONUT BREAD

I have a sweet tooth and if I had my way, every meal would begin with some type of sugar component. What I love about this banana and coconut bread recipe is that my girls have helped me make it since they were tiny, so it has lots of happy memories for us! It's also a quick and easy way to get rid of those brown bananas that can clutter up your fruit bowl. The recipe is courtesy of style and food guru Paula Joye.

Ingredients
⅓ cup melted butter
3 large ripe bananas (smashed)
1 cup brown sugar
1 beaten egg
1 tsp vanilla
1 tsp baking soda
pinch of salt
1½ cups of all-purpose flour
⅓ cup of shredded coconut, plus shredded coconut to sprinkle

Method
No need for a mixer for this recipe, which is another winning ingredient for me! Preheat the oven to 175 degrees Celsius. With

a wooden spoon, mix melted butter into the mashed bananas in a large mixing bowl.

Next, mix in the sugar, egg and vanilla. Sprinkle the baking soda and salt over the mixture and mix in. Add the flour and coconut and mix.

Pour mixture into a buttered 10 × 20 cm (4 × 8 inch) loaf pan. Bake for 1 hour.

Cool on a rack. Remove from pan and slice to serve.

Success rate

Four out of four family members love this! It's also delicious toasted and served with lots of butter. Just be sure to slice it nice and thickly so it pops out of the toaster without getting stuck! I've wasted too much time over the years upending toasters to budge stubborn bits of bread!

9

Mental Health

Listen, I wish I could tell you it gets better but it
doesn't get better. You get better.

JOAN RIVERS

Holding back my tears each day until I got into the relative privacy of my car after work was a warning sign. Most
days I could wait until reaching the relative safety of my
jam-packed car—full of my own clothes, a few pairs of
work shoes, water bottles, empty takeaway coffee cups
and missing blue school jumpers—before I would burst
into tears. However, this past week, my tears had begun
soon after I left the producer's office and walked across
the open-plan newsroom. Some of my work colleagues saw
those tears streaming down my face as I hurried quickly
downstairs to the carpark.

Sure, we all have our bad days, especially when things don't go our way, but I was frightened about revisiting those terribly dark days that I had experienced when I had postnatal depression. It had been such a struggle to manage my anxiety and panic attacks and I didn't want to disappear down that hole of despair again. I recognised that what I was now experiencing was different to PND but some of the symptoms of anxiety and depression were making their ugly presence felt once again and I didn't want to make room for those destructive emotions. Deep in my heart I knew that if I didn't make some drastic changes to my life, I would fall apart.

#CRAPHOUSEWIFE

'Pussycat, how was the show . . . ?' asked Peter, who would always call me at the same time each day, knowing that I'd be off air and in the car driving home.

'Okay . . .' I replied in a muffled voice.

Peter knew that when I said 'okay' it actually meant 'terrible'.

Other times, I would get weepy talking to my good friend and manager DW, who realised I was also just hanging in there by the tip of my shellac nails. I didn't like the person I was turning into: someone who complained and blamed everyone else for my exhaustion. Also, it was getting harder to ignore my growing resentment and my increasingly dark moods and tears.

Other times I'd cry in the dressing-room I shared with Neesy. She would hug me, even though she's not a hugger, and tell me that no job was ever worth getting that upset about.

'Just fuck them!' she said, knowing that I wasn't a fan of swearing but knew that I'd laugh at the flourish with which she said the f word! And she was right; it wasn't worth risking my mental health or happiness for the sake of an 'entertaining' argument on a morning panel show.

#CRAPHOUSEWIFE

On the outside, I had it all together: a happy family, the dream job that I had finally landed in the media, fabulous friends and our cats. But we all know that nothing is ever what it seems and I was managing to keep up appearances thanks to my morning dose of antidepressants. Despite the medication, I recognised that my daily tears and exhaustion were a sign that I needed to make some big, brave changes. It was time to do more than just fall into a heap every Friday night before then fortifying myself for another week at work. Thankfully, our family had a financial safety net, which meant I had no more excuses for making a sea change. No more procrastinating as I knew I needed to be more present and emotionally consistent with my girls and husband. It was time for me to make that big, bold leap into the deep blue.

All of us are influenced by our own upbringing; whether we want to emulate our parents, do it totally differently, or use a combination of these approaches when it comes to raising our own family. For me, I wanted to mix the wondrous bravery of my mother, the kindness of my stepfather, the enthusiasm of my father, the pragmatism of my stepmother along with my own energetic, eccentric approach. My own daughters—strong, stubborn souls—were on the cusp of their teenage years and it wouldn't be long before they wouldn't want me around cramping their style. It was time for me to more tightly weave those connections of love, self-esteem, confidence and self-worth before the girls took full flight into those risky, rebellious years.

#CRAPHOUSEWIFE

When my girls were tiny I used to think I had to be 'happy' all the time. My constantly cheerful mummy routine had been a reaction to growing up with a mum whose bipolar disorder meant her mood plummeted for months at a time into the howling depths of despair, regardless of what was happening in our lives. Now, as a parent, I found it exhausting having to keep up the constant tap-dancing routine for my children. Over the years I've had professional help to deal with how I manage my emotions, which has in turn helped me to be a better parent. What I learnt during these sessions was the value of regulating my emotional behaviour for me and my girls. I discovered it has been much more important to show my girls natural, emotional responses to the vagaries of life. How would my girls learn how to regulate their own emotions if I wasn't showing them the usual responses to happy, sad, boring, glorious, terrible or just okay situations?

Sometimes it's hard not to fall back on those 'bad' habits since I'm still working on undoing a lifetime of putting on a brave face. My self-cast role from when I was a little girl was to be 'Miss Cheerful'. Naively, I had thought that if I remained sunny and upbeat, that would be enough to 'fix' my beautiful mother. If I was good enough, happy enough, funny enough and caring enough then this would make her better. One of the first times I realised that Mum wasn't 'like other mothers', I was about ten years old. Her bedroom was right next to mine, the walls not thick enough to muffle the cries that got louder and louder. Frightened, I crept out of my single bed and walked to Mum's closed bedroom door, staring at the doorknob, wondering if I should open it. Frozen in that position, I was torn between opening the door to comfort her or sneaking back to bed. Eventually, I decided to sit against her door, still and quiet. Each night I couldn't move from that spot until the anguished sounds on the other side of the door had stopped; only then would I go back to my bed and sleep. I never asked Mum about those noises in the night. The smiling, happy mother I knew in the waking hours was so different to the woman I heard behind her closed door once the stars had come out to brighten the night sky. At the age of ten I was obsessed with ballet and chocolate Monte biscuits, and I had already learnt about putting on a brave face to survive.

This gift of hiding my emotions became perfect training for my media career where it's important to be consistent, calm and cheerful regardless of whatever else is happening in your life. This cheerfulness I wore like an armour, which was good professional protection but it did nothing to help me when I was at my most vulnerable. I couldn't take off that armour to ask for help when I needed it most. And the pressure to keep wearing that 'happy face' only increased after realising I had postnatal depression after Allegra's birth. Incorrectly, I had believed that it was a sign of weakness to admit that I was struggling as a new mum. No one knew how sick I was in those early months of motherhood as I hid the real me from myself, my husband, my mum and my friends.

Allegra was the only one I would whisper to in the dead of night.

'I love you, my darling, my beauty, my everything. You know how much Mummy loves you. I'm sorry that I can't breastfeed you properly. I'm sorry that I'm not a good mummy. I'm sorry that I'm so frightened about what will happen to you. I love you, I love you.'

#CRAPHOUSEWIFE

During the gruelling IVF process, I'd made a pact with myself never to complain if I was going to be blessed with a baby of my own. How I used to hate over-hearing those women in the coffee shop whingeing about how 'hard' it was with a new baby, when I thought they should have been rejoicing at their natural ability to be mothers. The cocktail of hormones pumping through my body during each IVF cycle would play havoc with my usually calm mood. Even those happy family stick-figure stickers on the back of cars, mainly four-wheel drives, would set me off. What right did these people have to flaunt their fertility? How dare they brag about the number of children, cats, dogs, skateboards and surf-boards they were lucky enough to 'own'? Quickly, my mood would swing from weepy, resentful anger to a full-blown psychotic rage.

And now that I had my baby, I was struggling behind this thickening pane of glass between me and the rest of the world. One of my strengths had always been my ability to connect but now all I could feel was numbness and shame. How dare I be so afraid, anxious and wretched when I had everything I had always wanted: my husband, my baby girl, my little family?

Gazing into my baby girl's blue eyes, I told her how lucky I was to have her.

'You have always been my wish upon a star. Although you are here now, you have always been here in my heart. I'm doing my best, my baby girl.'

#CRAPHOUSEWIFE

I had been looking forward to going to Mothers' Group and connecting with some like-minded new mums. I remember being the last one to arrive at the baby clinic. Struggling to push open the door, I tried to balance Allegra in her baby capsule on one arm and lug a huge bag on the other, crammed full of wipes, dummies, disposable nappies, a leopard-print change mat, spare clothes for Allegra and breast pads. The breast pads were an optimistic addition, as I had struggled to breastfeed properly since Allegra was born and my nipples were cracked and bleeding!

Sighing noisily as I came into the room, I glanced at the other mothers already in the group. None of them looked flustered or sweaty and I was betting they'd had no problems getting their baby capsules into the car. They were all sitting in a circle, blissfully breastfeeding and snuggling their babies. I found the last chair in the circle at the back of the room and placed Allegra at my feet in her capsule, happily sucking on her pink dummy.

'You're not using that, are you?' said the nurse running the group.

'Yes, it's helping me with settling Allegra. And she really likes it.'

'No, no, that's no good. She won't be able to latch on properly for feeding. You can't rely on that.'

I looked around the group of women, holding back my tears. A few of their babies had dummies as well. Surely it wasn't that bad?

'Isn't this the best thing you've ever done?' asked one mother.

'It just gets better and better,' replied another.

Christ. Next, I'll hear that they orgasm while breast-feeding.

'Oh, and I just love breastfeeding.'

I stayed silent. *No, this is not the best thing I have ever done,* I thought. *It is the worst thing I have ever done.* I didn't know what I was doing. I loved my baby girl but it was excruciatingly painful to breastfeed. I couldn't collapse the pram. I was using dummies, formulas and bottles. And it wasn't getting better, it was getting worse. I couldn't sleep even though I had never been so dog-tired in my life. I felt out of control, scared and overwhelmed. And I shouldn't have been feeling like this. I had wanted to have this glorious, golden baby for such a long time and now it was such a struggle to have her. It should have been the happiest time of my life and I should have been grateful. All the women in this group looked calm and capable— not like me. But I kept my chirpy veneer in place, nodded my head and smiled. I would not be coming back to this meeting. I'm sure that on the surface I looked like I was coping and, in hindsight, there would have been some other mums in that group who, like me, were drowning— floating adrift, desperate to be thrown a lifeline.

I had never been more alone. Somehow I had fantas- ised that I would find my girl gang at this meeting. Surely I wasn't the only mother who was struggling? What was wrong with me? I had been too scared to open up in front of these women, who seemed to wear their motherhood like a badge of honour in a competition they were winning. I had always been so in control of my life and believed that by working hard at something it would turn out the right way. But I had never worked harder at anything and been so powerless over the outcome. I was not winning this mothering caper. And I couldn't tell anyone.

My PND crept up on me, along with a combination of factors that created the perfect storm for my mental illness. I was a perfectionist, I had struggled to conceive, I couldn't breastfeed, I got sacked from my job and I had a long family history of mental illness. Now I cannot point to just one of these factors as being more significant than another, but looking at that list, it makes absolute sense that I had postnatal depression.

What does PND look like? I'm not a medical expert but what I'll do is describe what the illness was like for me and how it affected my life. Soon after Allegra was born I had a sense that my anxiety about what might happen to her was way out of whack with the normal level of worries that you would expect to have as a new mother. An example of this was the way I fixated on my failure to breastfeed my newborn daughter. I had equated those difficulties (and I persisted for far too long with trying to breastfeed properly) with being a terrible mother who would starve her daughter because she couldn't even manage the supposedly easy job of breastfeeding! I had been brainwashed in the maternity hospital that 'breast was best' and I had convinced myself that I would never be able to do the best for my daughter.

There was a gradually thickening pane of glass between me and the rest of the world, and initially I thought I could ignore it and simply blame it on exhaustion. However the world kept living, breathing and laughing without me in it. I had been tempted to confide in my sisters, my mum and Peter but I was fearful about giving my anxieties oxygen. I hadn't been ready to admit my fears to myself and I wrongly believed that if they stayed in my head, perhaps my thoughts would disappear. Putting a voice to my anxieties might make them appear all too real and I didn't know how I would manage that. Adrift, my mind started to stray further and further from the reality and routine of my days. And the days were never-ending; the time between dusk and dawn and dawn and dusk seemed endless. I stumbled through, dividing my day into two- and three-hourly feeding slots as well as changing, snuggling and settling Allegra back to sleep.

During this time, Peter had been travelling overseas a lot for his job as a reporter for *60 Minutes* so that made it easier for me to hide my growing anxiety. I couldn't admit to him I was a failure, and that I was letting him, our baby and our brand-new family down. How could I tell him what I was feeling? I was ashamed and drowning in guilt. How could I confess that I was falling apart when

I had finally achieved my fairy-tale ending? I started to have panic attacks for the first time in my life and I fixated more and more on my inability to breastfeed. And I also started to isolate myself, finding it easier to hide my fears behind my closed front door.

#CRAPHOUSEWIFE

The only thing I kept doing during this time was walking the streets with my sister Harriet, the pair of us pushing our babies in their prams. Somehow I thought this would keep me connected with the outside world and I could walk my way through the fear, pretence and anxiety. Some days when the sunlight warmed my face and brought colour to my cheeks, I believed I had managed to keep the vampires from the door. I grabbed those moments, hoping they would lengthen into an hour or two. But once I closed the door, no light came through. I was stuck, trapped, observing the world without me taking part in it.

I had seen what had happened to my mother when it was all too much, and certainly some part of me was fearful that I might end up in a psychiatric ward. My mind was making all sorts of catastrophic leaps and I was terrified about where it would end. The skill set and default mechanism that had got me through my 36 years wasn't working anymore. What I really needed to do was ask for help but instead, I kept up my award-winning performance as the perfect mother with the perfect baby.

It was getting harder and harder to keep up my daylight performance. When the phone rang, I didn't want to pick it up, detesting the false cheeriness in my voice when I answered. After a while I stopped returning calls from my girlfriends. I didn't want to talk to anyone, so it was easier to let the phone keep ringing. I kept writing down 'useful' information in a large diary. There was so much to remember, so much to write down, because I had to make sure I was doing everything the 'right' way. I had to get it all down on paper before I could get any sleep. What side had I finished feeding Allegra on? Was my breast drained of milk? And if it wasn't properly drained, would I get mastitis again? Did Allegra have a wet or dry nappy? How long had she slept for? Was it time to wake her up yet? How did I know how long to feed her for? I remembered that one of the midwives at the hospital had told me I should feed for at least fifteen minutes on each breast.

I would gaze at the silver Tiffany clock on the side table and watch the second hand go tick, tick, tick. Time slowed down, dragging its silver hand through pain, blood and tears. Why didn't Allegra open her mouth wide enough so I could feed her? How could I get her to attach properly? What was wrong with me? Why couldn't I do it? Both my mother and the paediatrician had encouraged me to use formula as a way to make sure that Allegra was putting on enough weight. I did start to use formula to 'top up' the breastfeeding; however, I thought this was yet another sign of how I was a failure.

The relentless soundtrack of 'guilty, bad mother' kept whirling around and around in my head. What right did I have to feel like this? I had plenty of support around me. A caring, extended family who often came around for visits, bringing supplies of good coffee and ready-made meals. Christina mopped the floors and scrubbed the bathroom so the house was tidy. We weren't battling to pay the mortgage or put food on the table. I had it easy—nothing to complain about.

#CRAPHOUSEWIFE

Coincidentally, during this time I had been contacted by beyondblue, the support organisation for sufferers of mental illness, asking if I would be prepared to accept a role as patron of its perinatal program. The timing of the call was extraordinary because the organisation's representative had no idea I was struggling with my sanity. No one did. Mum and I had done a lot of advocacy work for beyondblue over the years and it was ironic that much of this work had involved public speaking, sharing the message that there should be no shame or stigma attached to mental illness. And here I was, burning with that very shame. I confirmed that I would love to help out and asked for some further information.

Here was the checklist of symptoms for postnatal depression (PND) that arrived from beyondblue.

If you have experienced some of the following symptoms for two weeks or more, it's time to get help:

- low mood and/or feeling numb
- feeling inadequate, like a failure, guilty, ashamed, worthless, hopeless, helpless, empty or sad
- often feeling close to tears
- feeling angry, irritable or resentful (e.g. feeling easily irritated by your other children or your partner)
- fear for the baby and/or fear of being alone with the baby or the baby being unsettled
- fear of being alone or going out
- loss of interest in things that you would normally enjoy
- recurring negative thoughts—'I'm a failure', 'I'm doing a bad job', 'My life is terrible'
- insomnia (being unable to fall asleep or get back to sleep after night feeds) or excessive (too much) sleep, having nightmares
- appetite changes (not eating or over-eating)
- feeling unmotivated and unable to cope with a daily routine

- withdrawing from social contact and/or not looking after yourself properly
- having thoughts about harming yourself or your baby, ending your life, or wanting to escape or get away from everything

If you're having these kinds of thoughts, it's important to seek support.

I had answered yes to most of these questions but it was hard to accept that this meant I had PND. That soundtrack kept whirring around in my head. What did I have to be miserable about? I was one of the lucky ones. I wasn't a single mum, or struggling financially. And I had a wardrobe full of fabulous shoes. But none of this made the pane of glass go away. I told myself to get over it. I hid the beyondblue booklet in my top drawer, thinking that would silence the negative thoughts. Close it up, lock it away, shut up. Everything will be alright.

But it wasn't alright. There was something about the dead of night during that time that still chills me. I used to hate sitting on the couch trying to breastfeed while outside it was pitch-black, not a star in the sky. The only sound I could hear was the ticking of the silver clock, the second hand not moving fast enough to get me away from the scary night-time world. I would wrap my baby girl up into her parcel of love and lay her back into her cot. Such a good girl, she would slip off to sleep quickly. But I would return to bed full of dread, knowing that I would lie there for hours unable to sleep. Every pore of my body would want to drift off into a gentle cottonwool sleep. Instead, my brain would not switch off. I would be high on adrenaline, buzzy and wired and unable to turn off the thoughts whizzing around and around in my head. All I could do was think, think, think. Tick, tick, tick.

Each night I watched the clock hand creep around as I stroked the top of my darling daughter's head. I would look at that perfectly round clock and ponder about how easily it could smash my daughter's skull, worrying about how it could slip from the table and the damage it could cause ... all while Allegra slept happily and innocently through the night.

Then I would start thinking about the carving knife in the second drawer in the kitchen. It could so easily pierce my daughter's delicate skin. My mind kept returning to the wooden handle of the knife, its long blade. I was losing my mind. It got to the point where I didn't want to go through another night with these thoughts and it wasn't long before they snuck into the daytime too. Tick, tick, tick.

One morning, desperate to delete this frightening loop in my head, I decided to wrap up the knife in old newspaper and throw it away along with the other rubbish in our large garbage bin. I thought getting rid of the knife would quieten the disturbing power of these obsessive thoughts. Creeping out of bed before sunrise, I managed to throw the knife into the bin without making a sound. What had become of me?

But the daylight wasn't enough to save me. I knew there was something very wrong. Would I have to go to hospital? Would my baby be taken from me? Would the pane of glass pierce my body and make me bleed?

After another terrible night with these thoughts, I realised that I couldn't keep going and that I had to ask for help. The first person I turned to was my mother, as I knew she would understand. Mum listened and reassured me that I would get through this but she made me promise her that I would tell Peter and that I would talk to my doctor. And talking to my husband was one of the hardest things I've ever had to do in my life.

#CRAPHOUSEWIFE

'You are going so well. I am so proud of you,' Peter said after we had finished eating our dinner in front of the television.

I had cooked Peter's favourite meal of schnitzel and mashed potato (but this was long before I discovered panko crumbs). A rocky road chocolate bar was waiting in the fridge for dessert. I knew this was my moment, my time to say something. Tick, tick, tick.

'I'm not,' I blurted out. 'I'm not coping. I'm afraid I have postnatal depression. I am so, so sorry.' Tears ran down my face.

Peter was silent for a moment then he looked at me, his clear blue eyes filled with worry.

'You're not going to hurt yourself, are you?'

'No,' I replied.

'You're not going to hurt Allegra? Promise me you wouldn't hurt her?' he said urgently.

'No. No!'

I *knew* I would never hurt my baby, but I couldn't tell Peter about the thoughts in my head just yet.

Peter took me in his arms and held me tight while I buried my face in his shoulder.

'I know what we'll do.'

He had already slipped into his fix-it mode.

'I'll ring Jan, the obstetrician, tomorrow and you can go in and talk to her. It's okay. It's going to be okay.'

For the first time in a long time I felt safe. I needed to hear those words of reassurance from my husband. He didn't judge me or tell me that I was being ridiculous or imagining things. He had heard me and my cry for help that night. And that simple act of telling him took some of the heavy weight off my shoulders.

#CRAPHOUSEWIFE

Once I had asked for help, I was lucky to get the right help straight away. Firstly, I poured my heart out to our obstetrician, who had already organised for me to see a psychiatrist who specialised in PND the very next day. I had finally given voice to my black thoughts and as they bounced against the glass, they lost some of their fierceness.

I had dressed very carefully for my meeting with the psychiatrist, choosing a brown cotton fifties-style dress with a diamond pattern, silver glitter ballet flats and pink lipstick. Once I sat down opposite her, the first thing she told me was that I could 'stop pretending now'. Some more weight lifted off my shoulders. Then I told her about my worries for Allegra, my problems with breastfeeding, losing my job, Mum's illness and my scary obsessive thoughts.

'But that's normal,' the doctor replied.

'Normal—what? It's normal to have images of clocks and knives going around on a constant loop in your brain?'

'Yes, it is normal for someone who has postnatal depression,' she continued. 'Obsessive, unpleasant thoughts are very common in people with PND.'

'I would never hurt Allegra.'

'I know that.'

'And I would never hurt myself.'

'I know that.'

'So why is it happening to me? Where have these thoughts come from?'

'Because your mind has been working in a panicked and anxious state, normal objects that you deal with every day can start to become sinister,' she explained. 'You start misinterpreting things that you have used for a long time without having any problems. Because of the way your brain has been working, such objects start to appear hazardous and dangerous to your baby. The world becomes a very scary place because you want to do everything to protect your child—you are so intent on looking after her and keeping her safe that everywhere you look, there is danger.'

'So, I'm not a crazy lady?'

'No, but you do have an illness: postnatal depression.'

Desperate to get better, I had no problems with my psychiatrist's advice to start on medication combined with regular appointments. On the way home from that first appointment I stopped off at the pharmacy to get the antidepressants. I marked the date down in my diary with a star as I swallowed my first tablet.

I remember standing on our front lawn just two weeks later and the scent of jasmine in the breeze—the sweet, heady smell of summer—tickled my nose and made me sneeze. Oh how I love this fragrance; it makes me think of sand, sunshine, hot concrete, lemonade icy poles and cool blue water. I hadn't smelt that sweet scent in such a long time, even though the vines had been flowering along our back fence since I had brought Allegra home from the hospital.

With that scent came a flickering deep inside of me, like a butterfly beating its wings. What was it? It felt like hope. A change in the wind, a chance to breathe out and exhale just a little more. And as I took a breath, I felt like I was returning to myself again. The dead of night was frightening me less and less. My obsessive thoughts started to fade to grey, until they totally disappeared. And I kissed the top of Allegra's soft, sweet head, inhaling her very essence.

My recovery from PND wasn't instantaneous; it took time, patience with myself, medication and the love of my family and tight tribe of friends. And I realised that I was at a higher risk of having it again once I was pregnant with our second child. But the next time around I was determined to be gentler on myself and ask for help sooner if I needed it. Through my second pregnancy, I saw my psychiatrist on a regular basis and we talked about not putting so much pressure on myself. I organised hands-on help for when I brought Giselle home and I wasn't going to let myself be bullied into breastfeeding. There were no anxiety or panic attacks but what did appear again was that familiar, stubborn pane of glass, still separating me from the sunshine and the rest of the world. But I didn't ignore it and restarted my medication, which made that glass disappear.

Having PND had been a hard lesson, but it taught me about bravery and courage; that it's a sign of strength and not weakness to ask for help. I got better because I asked for help. And that is what resonates with me in the wise-cracking words of comedian Joan Rivers. Here was a woman who had her fair share of sadness, struggle and chutzpah in her life. Having a mental illness has also taught me that perfection is impossible, and our flaws are what make us beautiful and human. It has also shown me the power of connecting through our stories, and since sharing my story of PND I have been humbled by the number of women who have also told me about their own struggles. Each and every one of us wears a mask or armour but I've learnt that since dropping my armour, I've been able to embrace and revel in my imperfection and vulnerability. I love being flawed and fabulous. And we're all still works in progress.

The experience also taught me to look after my own mental health, which doesn't always have to be as extreme as quitting your job. There are also less drastic ways to stay on track and for me, that includes getting enough sleep, exercise and mindfulness. I've never been a fitness fanatic and I don't believe the words 'fun' and 'run' should ever go together. Over the years I've dabbled in weight training, which was perfect for both my mental fitness and keeping my core super strong before, during and after my pregnancies. But more recently I've been doing Pilates, which stretches my body and mind and the best part is that I go along with my friend Pip. The pair of us laugh, trying not to disrupt the rest of the class, and because we go together we're more likely to turn up. However, I'm still desperately trying not to fart in my activewear while I bounce off the jump board trying to work out if I'm squeezing the right muscles or not! My instructor has told me to imagine I'm drinking a cocktail through a straw up my bottom! I laugh, trying to visualise drinking an Aperol Spritz like that—and that is another reason why I love Pilates.

Mindfulness is another technique I use for keeping my head together. For a long time this buzz word annoyed me as I pushed back against the new age-ness of it. My mind was never still enough for yoga and, stupidly, I used to lump sugar-free, chakras and coconut oil in with mindfulness. However, the breakthrough for me was comedian Ruby Wax's book: *Sane New World*. Her humour, honesty and simple tips about how to simplify your life and deal with that negative loop in your head were game changers. Now I never walk through a doorway without realising that I'm walking through a door!

I talk to my own daughters about times when I've been deeply sad or struggled to manage my emotions. I speak to them about my dark times when they were tiny but I keep telling them that although Mummy's brain was sad, they never, ever made me sad and it was their light that kept me fighting to get back into the sunshine. I teach them that it's okay to sometimes be sad and those feelings only sweep through us and don't remain stuck inside. But if it does feel like they're stuck, let's talk about ways we can get those feelings out. And I tell them that one way I manage my emotions is by taking tablets for 'my brain'. However, Allegra is more concerned that I keep taking the pill 'that stops you from having any more babies, Mummy'. She's not keen on having any more sisters or a brother . . .

CHICKEN PIE

This recipe is from the genius *4 Ingredients: One Pot, One Bowl* cookbook. I'm a huge fan of Kim McCosker's no-fuss, 'so simple even a crap housewife can make it' approach to cooking.

Ingredients
2 sheets puff pastry

1 barbecue chicken

1 can condensed cream of chicken soup (or you can use condensed cream of mushroom soup)

500 g frozen mixed vegetables (sometimes I'll leave the veggies out as my youngest daughter won't eat them!)

Method
Preheat oven to 180 degrees Celsius. Defrost the 2 puff pastry sheets. Line pie dish with baking paper and 1 sheet of pastry.

Remove all the chicken meat from the barbecue chook.

Next, in a bowl, combine the soup, chicken and veggies (cook the frozen veggies before you add them to the mix so they won't go soggy during the baking process).

Pour mixture into the pie dish and then cover with the other piece of pastry. Squish the edges of the pastry together so it looks neat and tidy! Cut some slits in the pie lid. You could also whisk an egg and paint it over the top of the pastry sheet to help the pastry become nice and golden during the cooking process. I also like to use any leftover pastry to make the outline of a heart or my girls' initials to put on top of the pie.

Bake it in the oven for 30–35 minutes. Once it's golden brown—voila!

You could serve the pie with mashed potatoes or a salad.

Success rate

Perfect score! Four out of four family members eat this.

10

Mothering

My mother had a great deal of trouble with me,
but I think she enjoyed it.

MARK TWAIN

'Mumma, sing me a song. Sing what you sang to me when I
was a baby', said Giselle, as I stretched across her to switch
off her pink bedside lamp. We'd just finished reading a
chapter of her latest book from the school library.

'Hush, little baby, don't say a word, Mumma's going
to buy you a mocking bird! If that mocking bird don't
sing, Mumma's going to buy you a diamond ring. If that
diamond ring don't sparkle, Mumma's going to buy you
a horse and, um, cart-el . . .' I sang hesitantly.

'That's random. Sparkle doesn't rhyme with horse and
cart, Mumma,' said Giselle, quick as a flash.

The pair of us laughed as I told my daughter I had no idea what the correct words were for this lullaby. We decided to stick with 'Incy Wincy Spider', as those words I did remember!

Only a few years earlier I had known all of the words to these lullabies but as my eldest daughter starts to grow taller than me, and Giselle's not far behind, those days of when she and her sister were small seem like a lifetime ago. I used to inwardly groan when older, more knowing (smug) parents would advise me: 'Don't miss a moment. It goes in the blink of an eye.' These comments would sting, especially after a tricky day when I had wanted to disappear in the blink of an eye! Surely there's nothing wrong with that and besides, I'm still on the lookout for my own fast-forward button.

#CRAPHOUSEWIFE

There is so much I still don't know about being a mother. But what I've learnt is that there is not a one-size-fits-all way of being a good-enough mum. For me, I'm now so much gentler on myself compared to when my girls were babies. My youngest daughter has 'missed out' on going to the playgrounds where I would have taken her big sister. I had been going brain dead at the park and the thought of spending any more time in grotty sandpits than was necessary filled me with dread. However, as my confidence grew, I realised I didn't have to keep going to the playground! Who was I trying to impress? Instead, I found more joy choosing to do things that were fun for me too; like doing dress-ups, colouring in, listening to the birdsongs of our local magpies, pointing out the rainbow lorikeets as well as the tailless lizards who had managed to escape from our cats.

The breastfeeding that had been part of my downfall in the early days of motherhood came much easier the second time around. I had learnt to speak up and wasn't going to allow myself to be pushed around in the hospital by the bossy but well-meaning midwives. This time I wasn't going to go home with bleeding and cracked nipples. Each day, I threw back the curtains in my hospital room to stay connected with the wider world. And I also asked sooner for help from family and friends once I got home with my baby girl. I was learning that asking for help was a sign of strength. No one can—or should—do it on their own.

Where does the hum of anxiety that surrounds being a modern-day mum come from? I've spoken with our first female governor general Dame Quentin Bryce about this issue facing many parents. For her, the topic has come up frequently in the conversations she has had with families over the years. Dame Quentin says it often comes back to how they find it 'hard going working out how to be a very good parent'. She thinks it's because life has become more complex. For example, there are now more step-families, there's the internet to contend with, plus the fact that many parents are older.

She says that another problem for mothers today is the lack of community in many of our suburbs. It's a world where our neighbours are very often strangers. 'A lot of the suburbs are empty now. I drive in them. I see them. I don't see a child on the footpath and I don't see kids playing cricket at the end of the road.'

In contrast, when she was a young mother, Quentin remembers a 'carefree environment' in the street where her family lived. 'My next-door neighbours would bring my washing in if it looked like rain, and they would fold it up. And I had wonderful neighbours around everywhere.'

The internet isn't all bad and the challenge is to filter out the online nonsense that can make you feel inad-equate, such as many of those parenting, fitness and food blogs. Twitter had been a lifeline when I was stuck at home with my baby girls, as its catchy, short stream of conversation, gossip and news helped me feel connected to the wider world. Also thanks to the net, our genera-tion has never had more information, articles, websites and manuals about being a good parent. We've never been more present for our children. It's time to back our own abilities when it comes to our kids, as no one knows our children better than we do. If you want to feed them some sugar, have dinner in front of the telly and allow them to get on their devices every now and then, just do it.

But this knowledge hasn't helped to quieten that nagging fear that we're not 'getting it right'. Why do we do this to ourselves? Why are we such tough taskmasters? Are we putting way too much pressure on ourselves to 'have it all'? Yes. Are we fearful of not being perfect? Yes. Generally, I'm getting much better at being more flexible with the choices I make for our family. My philosophy is: 'Do whatever gets you through that moment, day or night!' And since putting that into practice, I'm far more confident in my mothering 'skills' and making choices based on what works for me and my family.

Now I'm more willing to change things that don't work, regardless of what some book or expert says I 'should' be doing. What do I mean by this? Okay, I've learnt to pick my battles with my children. It doesn't matter if they don't brush their hair, wear the same outfit, or want to eat the same food for weeks on end. But I won't tolerate rudeness or bad manners. It's okay if they bicker with one another (although it's so boring to listen to, and I don't care who started it). But it is not okay to be unkind to one another, as kindness and compassion matter a lot to our family. These big-ticket items are the battles worth fighting for.

Although we are now missing that sense of community that many of our parents experienced growing up in their neighbourhoods, I'm not convinced that families were necessarily any better off during that 'golden age' compared with today. Were families any happier, were children any better behaved? Or was it simply that we didn't talk about postnatal depression, anxiety and those other tough topics during those supposed halcyon times? Many of us survived our childhood purely through good luck and benevolent neglect from our less-than-present parents. There were no seatbelts and I remember sliding around on the prickly carpet in the boot of my dad's Mini Minor. We rode our bicycles without helmets along our back laneway, unsure of how to use the pedal brakes, and stopped only by crashing into the long, itchy grass at the bottom of the hill. We were often left to our own devices; making up endless ABBA concerts and writing handbooks for secret clubs based on the Famous Five novels.

I haven't been able to convince my daughters of the delights of reading the Famous Five but I'm still trying to turn them into ABBA fans by pumping 'Dancing Queen' through my car's sound system, if I can get them to turn off Cardi B or Nicki Minaj. And the older my girls get, the more I enjoy spending time with them. It's not as if

I love them any more or less, it's simply more fun being with them and discovering the people they're growing into. It's hard to articulate the never-ending, all-encompassing, aching love that I have for my girls.

'Mumma, how much do you love me?' asks Giselle at least once a week.

'More than all the moons and stars in the sky, to the Milky Way and beyond, my Baby Bear,' I reply, after adding some more words to another lullaby and before kissing her goodnight.

'Do you love me the most?' she asks, with her cheeky smile.

'I love you *and* your sister the most.'

'But I'm your favourite, aren't I, Mumma?'

'You are both my favourites . . .'

It's impossible to have a favourite child but it's not impossible to have a favourite time for being with your children. And for me, my favourite moments are right now as my girls grow into little women. Quite simply, I had struggled with the sheer exhaustion and monotony of having babies. I have never been one of those women who goes weak at the sight of a newborn. Hearing that mewling cry still makes my insides seize up, and I'm relieved it's no longer my responsibility to feed and settle a baby. However, I've got friends who crave that soft, sweet smell of a brand-new baby. Sometimes the sight of them makes them want more children. That has never, ever been me! Even when I was pregnant with Giselle, I knew that two was my magic number.

Spending time with my growing girls is my priority. If I can get my eldest off her iPad, we talk about politics, fashion and why it would be a really dumb idea for her to name her own daughter 'Paris Versace Overton'.

'But Mum, I really love the Paris Hilton perfume that I bought from Chemist Warehouse,' said Allegra.

She also knows that I can't stand Paris Hilton (partly because her father has a crush on her!).

'There are much prettier names than Paris . . .' I replied.

'And I thought her middle name could be Versace, so she'll have something to talk to Donatella about when she meets her . . .'

'Donatella will be dead by the time your daughter grows up,' said Giselle from the back of the car.

I couldn't help laughing, as I nodded in agreement.

And it's the conversations, whether it's about Paris Hilton, boys, fashion or more significant issues like why anyone would be cruel to children or animals, that I relish having with them. Gradually, I'm realising that I need to stop talking *at* my girls and that I should talk *with* them more. It's astonishing what issues can come up when we give our kids the space to speak. A big lesson for me has been learning that silence doesn't always have to be filled up with chatter.

#CRAPHOUSEWIFE

I've also learnt that shouting doesn't solve anything. No one likes to be shouted at. What are we teaching our kids about managing their emotions if bigger and more powerful people start yelling at them when they misbehave? When the girls were toddlers I used to have a 'calming down mat'. The mat was an old pink and yellow bathmat, which was the shape of Cinderella's carriage. The idea was to put them on the mat when they started to have a meltdown instead of putting them into their room. It didn't work, as I spent too much time carrying them back onto the mat, which they would jump off the minute I put them onto it! Eventually, that mat spent more time in our messy cupboard under the stairs than under their chubby, little bottoms.

Over the years, I experimented with putting the girls into their bedrooms if they misbehaved. However, there was nothing in the manuals about what to do if your children kept coming out of their rooms. At my wits' end one afternoon, I found myself pulling on one side of the silver doorknob while my young daughter used all of her strength to pull on her side of the door to get out! Wrestling over the doorknob, I ended up jamming Giselle's weeny fingers in the door. She started sobbing hysterically and I burst into tears too, tired and guilty, as I comforted her in my lap. That was the last time I tried that form of 'discipline'.

Another time I remember Giselle pinching me to get my attention. I told her to stop it, but she kept pinching my arm. My tolerance was low, I hadn't been getting much sleep, and I pinched her sharply straight back.

'See that's how much it hurts when you pinch Mummy!' I said angrily.

Her little cat-shaped eyes filled with tears as she looked at me in horror.

'Oh, I'm sooooo sorry, Mummy didn't mean to hurt you!' I said, scooping my crying daughter into my arms. Then I lay Giselle back down onto the bed next to me, and while I was gazing into her eyes, she pinched me again! Yet another parenting fail and one that I can now laugh about.

Eventually, I realised that sometimes the best thing to do is to remove myself from situations when I feel my anger and frustration reaching boiling point. Many times I have gone to our bedroom and jammed my body against the door for a moment's peace. Taking deep breaths and having your own 'time out' can work wonders. There are moments when you can feel out of control and undone by the stubbornness and screams of such small souls. Even my husband, who is as cool as a cucumber, has been known to rip up our daughters' rewards chart for good behaviour when things haven't gone to plan!

Handing out advice has never been my style. Instead, what I'd like to do is share some suggestions that have helped me and my family.

- I've learnt to say sorry to my girls. Sorry for shouting, sorry for getting angry and sorry for not staying in control. Often it goes like this: 'Darling, Mumma is sorry for getting so cross. I didn't mean to shout. I'm tired and I'm not perfect.' Then we have a hug and get on with the rest of the day.
- Laugh, do silly walks and never lose your own inner child. If your little one wants your attention, give it to them. Sit on the floor with them and stop doing whatever you're doing. No child can ever have too much attention, love and hugs.
- No baby sleeps all night, especially when they're tiny. Small babies can be boring. Breastfeeding isn't for everyone. Formula can be a godsend and it doesn't lower your baby's IQ. You will get some sleep—one day.

- Your nipples can bleed. Dummies are fine, I've never seen a teenager using a dummy.
- It's okay to let your kids see you cry. But it's more important for them to see you laugh and using your imagination.
- Lose your smartphone once you get home, then it's harder to be tempted to check it when your kids are watching you. They're little sponges and model their behaviour on their parents. If you worry about your kids spending too much time on their devices, stop and think about how often you use your phone. But it's okay to lock yourself in the bathroom sometimes (if you can) and use your iPad for some peace and quiet.
- Buy a trampoline that you can zip up. That way your children are safely contained and you can sit on the lawn and watch them.
- Toast or cereal can be served as an evening meal.
- It's okay to have your kids in your bed—they will end up in their own beds one day.
- We're all human, we don't have all the answers and we're all simply making it up as we go along.

And remember, you are never, ever there yet. That is what makes life as a mother so glorious.

CHICKEN ENCHILADA CAKE

Mexican meals are always a hit with kids. Instead of serving up tacos (which are always popular), why not try this version of an enchilada? Who would think a Mexican savoury cake would work? Well it does, thanks to the clever folk at 4 Ingredients. This is another recipe from their *One Pot, One Bowl* cookbook. I'm a fan of this style of cooking since the cooking part is minimal!

Ingredients
1 enchilada kit (it's easier to buy one of these at the supermarket as it already has 8 corn tortillas plus enchilada sauce)
2 cups of shredded barbecued chook
1 bag of grated cheese (it could be tasty, mozzarella, pizza cheese—whichever you prefer)

Method
Preheat oven to 200 degrees Celsius. Line a 20 cm (8 inch) round cake tin with baking paper. (I have no idea how big my tin was so I don't think size matters here, as long as there's enough room for the tortilla).

Now it's time to layer upon layer—starting with tortilla then enchilada sauce then chicken then cheese. Then start your next layer starting again with the tortilla, and keep layering until you've used up all the ingredients.

Bake in the oven until the cheese is completely melted and the sauce is bubbling. This should take around 30 minutes.

Success rate

Three out of four family members enjoyed this Mexican meal! Isn't there always one 'No, I don't like it!' though?

11

Fashion

More is more and less is a bore.

IRIS APFEL

Clothes have always brought me such delight. Sparkles, sequins, satin, fringing, tulle, leopard print, faux fur, fiery red, blushing pink and all the colours of the rainbow burst out of my wardrobe. Each day I'll dress depending on my mood, or the mood I want to project onto the world. And that is the transformative power of fashion. It's not about the latest trend or forcing yourself into outfits that will never suit you—it's about wearing a costume for the day. For me fashion is simply playing dress-ups for grown-ups. And that is why I'm obsessed with the excess of accessories, oversized glasses and confidence of style icon Iris Apfel. I could never subscribe to Coco Chanel's advice to take one thing off before leaving the house. Add something more instead!

#CRAPHOUSEWIFE

'Pussycat, where are you going?' my husband asked as we walked out the door together.

This morning Peter was wearing his preferred uniform of Nike hoodie, shorts and a navy cap, and white sports shoes. In comparison, I was wearing a green, glittery jumper, light-indigo jeans and silver-sequinned sneakers. Already the rainbow lorikeets were cheekily spitting out their leftover nectar breakfast from the branches of the bright-red bottlebrush tree that stretches out over the roof of my car. I stepped gingerly over the remains of the bottle-brush, so the flowers wouldn't stain my sneakers.

Our daughters were already in the backseat, yelling for us to stop talking. It's interesting how quickly the tables had turned, as it had been only the day before that we were nagging them to get out the front door and into the car.

'I'm going exactly where you're going, Petee!' I laughed, as the pair of us carried our daughters' ridiculously heavy school backpacks to the car.

Although we share the same moral code, we are mis-matched on most of the more flippant things in life—he's the yin to my yang.

My fashion sense has always been amplified. On our second date I dressed as a mermaid, giving Peter heart palpitations for all the wrong reasons.

'You look, ah, breathtaking . . .' he stuttered, as I opened the door to my beachside unit.

He had done the gentlemanly thing, picking me up to take me to a birthday dinner with my family and friends. Especially brave given he had never met any of these people before, and I'm sure he had second thoughts when he saw my aquatic birthday outfit. My good friend Annebelle, who was also the wardrobe mistress at Channel Ten (where I was reading the news at the time), had made me a shimmering blue asymmetrical cocktail frock, with a giant sequinned flower, trailing blue-, green- and opal-coloured sequins stitched onto the top strap of the dress. Remember, this was the age of the *Sex and the City* TV series when Sarah Jessica Parker used to rock up with similarly styled giant flowers pinned all over her outfits.

Another friend Nikki, who was my favourite make-up artist, teamed blue eyeshadow, loose glitter and fabulous fake eyelashes to complement my birthday get-up. I loved my look and was excited that Peter would be joining the celebrations. I hadn't met a good man in a long time and despaired that I never would since all my friends were getting married, or already had long-term partners. Thankfully, Peter wasn't scared away by my over-the-top costume and he didn't sense my desperation. He also politely pretended not to hear my excited friends who frequently told me, in not such soft voices, that Peter was 'such a catch!' At this stage I don't think he believed in the magic of mermaids.

During our courtship I proceeded to shock, surprise and startle my conservative boyfriend. My outlandish outfits continued and he was happy to stand by my side in his uniform of jeans and a pink polo shirt. Although we've been married for over fifteen years, neither of us has shifted much in our sartorial style. He keeps it simple; dressing up in a blue Hugo Boss shirt and navy chinos and RM Williams boots, while I keep pushing the fashion envelope further with fringes of sequins, rainbow pleated skirts and green and pink faux fur jackets.

#CRAPHOUSEWIFE

Although I've always had a weakness for clothes, I don't have many high-end labels in my wardrobe. Fancy, logo-covered handbags have never been my style. Instead, I'd rather save up for a few cat-printed coats and dresses.

Peter still doesn't know how much I spent on a Miu Miu pink pussycat coat, even though I kept reassuring him that thanks to a fashion stylist friend I was getting a large discount on it. It had taken months of research to hunt down this distinctive pink, red and burgundy coat.

I had also been coveting a long, white Dolce & Gabbana dress that was covered in brown Bengal cats for many months before it was discounted online. Then I pounced for the purchase! It remains one of my favourite frocks and I wore it when I announced my resignation on air from *Studio Ten*. One of the conscientious wardrobe girls was adamant that I couldn't wear the dress because of the pattern being too 'over the top'. She was unaware of what I would be announcing on the television that morning and I was determined to wear a statement when I made my statement! I reassured her that I would deal with any heat from her superiors and promptly went into my dressing-room to get changed into my wondrous pussycat dress.

You don't need to spend a fortune on fashion, as the simple act of teaming heart-shaped glasses you might have found at a cheap chain store with a slick of bright lipstick tells the world that you're in a playful mood. Alternatively, even if you're not feeling particularly playful but you want to project that mood, sunnies and lipstick can help fortify you for the day ahead. Other times your grey marbled T-shirt, jeans and thongs might say, 'I'm all about comfort today'. Or you might say, 'Stop being such a tosser, Jessica.

It is, after all, only clothes!' However, it is never only clothes to me. My clothes have become the timelines for significant moments in my life. I've donated to charity all of the coral, blue and pink Diane von Furstenberg wrap dresses, the crisp white Armani shirts and floral-patterned Escada jackets that the Channel Nine's wardrobe department had bought for me during my time on the *Today* show. I've thrown out the outfits that I wore during my postnatal depression as I don't want to be cloaked in anything from that time. But I still have hanging in my wardrobe the maternity dress that I wore when I went into labour with Allegra. That is the power of clothes.

#CRAPHOUSEWIFE

My hair is also a part of my daily fashion costume. I've had short hair for almost 30 years and there is no way I would ever grow it long. The reasons behind keeping my hair short are threefold: I haven't got the patience to grow it, I wouldn't recognise myself with long hair and short hair has become my trademark. And the man responsible for that trademark is the same hairdresser I've had since I was in my twenties. His name is Pierre and it's the longest relationship I've ever had with a man. The screen icon Joan Crawford, who was a nightmare in many areas of her life, was, however, spot on in her praise of a good hairdresser.

'I think the most important thing a woman can have, next to talent, of course, is her hairdresser.'

And, boy, do I understand the importance of my hairdresser. Pierre and I catch up every six weeks or so and, like most significant relationships, it began with a good opening line: 'Your hair looks terrible. I could do a much better job.'

Pierre was a friend of one of my boyfriends, and a group of us had gone to dinner at a cool pizza restaurant in Bondi. It was the first time I'd ever eaten a caprese salad and I wasn't sure about the gooey texture of the buffalo mozzarella.

'Umm, okay then . . . Give me your number. I'll call you,' I replied, hoping basil wasn't stuck in my teeth, slightly shocked by his honesty but most impressed by his cheek. All these years later, he still impresses me with his no-nonsense approach and dry, wry wit.

My hairdresser has been the one consistent man in my life. He has seen me through acne, university, heartache, marriage, IVF, pregnancy, depression, babies and career highs and lows.

Pierre humours me each time I sit down in his black leather swivel chair, as he knows exactly where our conversation will be heading because it's the same conversation each time.

'Let's talk about my hair . . .' I say.

'Let's not . . .'

'I would like a change.'

'No you don't. If you really wanted a change, you would grow it and what you really mean is that you just want your hair to be shorter.'

This man's a mind-reader as he knows that I've never had the inclination to grow my hair. And I love his honesty. He is always the first to tell me if I'm looking tired or if I need to keep those leopard-print harem pants for home.

Keeping my hair short has always appealed to the maverick in me and I've always managed to keep it short through my decades of working on television. Early on in my career, my ambition was clothed in pastel power suits and early morning starts in the newsroom, trying to get my stories of a cat stuck up a tree onto the evening news. However, some early signs of rebellion began to emerge with my choice of hairstyle. I resisted growing my short blonde hair into a 'broadcast bob', my description for that helmet of hair-sprayed, flicked, shoulder-length hair that many female TV presenters still wear on our television screens. One of my bosses had suggested growing my hair slightly longer so it would look 'softer and less severe' on the television. The next day I turned up with an even shorter haircut. He didn't dare ask me again to grow my hair. Over time I realised my short hair was a subtle, or at times not so subtle, way of thumbing my nose at conformity.

My hairdresser says the salon should be a place of 'relaxation and entertainment' and that he wants his clients to leave feeling better about themselves. Sure, for many of us it's about an aesthetic change but there have been plenty of times I've 'changed' my hair, hoping it will also help me on a deeper, more psychological level. I'm not the only woman who has gone to the hairdresser to wash that man right out of her hair. When I've broken up with boyfriends, I've changed my hairstyle. Believe me, there are many, many different ways to have short hair. Looking back through photos, I've had at least ten different short hairstyles over the years including: long fringe, the short fringe, the pixie, the buzz cut, the urchin, mini-mullet, the Mia Farrow, the punk, asymmetrical, and short and spikey . . .

When I was in the middle of postnatal depression and my career was in the doldrums, I decided to get my hair shaved and dyed platinum. When everything else was spiralling out of control, I thought that changing my hair would be a way to feel in control again, even if it was only for the 90 minutes that I was sitting in that leather chair. My buzz cut was a sign to myself that it was okay if I didn't fit the stereotype of what a 'good mum' was meant to look like. Or perhaps such a radical hair change had been part of my losing control before I could put myself back together again? I'm not sure, but I know that hairdressers are like therapists and they're cheaper than visiting a psychiatrist (I did make sure that I kept seeing my psychiatrist too).

#CRAPHOUSEWIFE

I've become captivated by a woman of an uncertain age who goes to the local salon. Each appointment she brings in the same silver framed wedding photo of herself from years ago, and asks her hairdresser to make her look like that. Then as she sits waiting for the dye to return her hair to its crowning glory, she sits in front of the mirror applying electric-blue liquid liner to her eyelids. Her time-warped look makes her feel like that young bride all over again. And if that makes her feel special, I'm all for it!

A visit to the hairdressing salon may be about recapturing your youth, a place to feel better about yourself, a place to go to have a laugh and a place where you think you'll be listened to since you have a captive audience in your hair stylist. However, here's a hint from a salon insider: if your hairdresser just says lots of 'Really?' 'That's amazing' 'No way' 'Then what happened?' and/or 'Are you crazy?' it means he or she isn't really listening . . .

I've always been a good listener, especially if there's a juicy conversation unfolding within my earshot. It's a talent I inherited from my mother and now my youngest daughter has turned out to be a champion eavesdropper too. And there is always plenty of gossip to uncover at the hairdressers. I've heard of a very fancy salon that kept a society couple's marriage together by preventing the wife from coming face to face with her husband's mistress each month. It took some fine penwork in the appointment book and some strategically placed mirrors, but the staff's thoughtful efforts have kept the dignity of this fine woman in place. The pair never had to meet up looking like bedraggled poodles over the washbasins. I understand that this détente went on for years, and everyone was able to keep up appearances.

Recently, I overheard a glamorous Carla Zampatti–clad woman telling her hairdresser that she felt invisible and that her husband didn't notice her anymore. She then went on to reveal she hadn't had an orgasm in twenty years of marriage. Perhaps there is something about sitting down in front of the salon mirror while the hairstylist wields his small silver scissors or best balayage technique that helps you to loosen your tongue.

Maybe it's the intimacy of having someone in your personal space, touching your hair, talking to you without looking directly into your eyes that creates such a miraculous truth serum. Hairdressers don't kiss and tell, so they know everything about you. The illicit liaisons, cosmetic surgery, the state of your mental health and the temperament of your cat(s). It can be tricky for some clients to hide those face-lift scars on their hairline when they're getting that fortnightly blow-dry. Indeed, my hairdresser was the first person to notice I had botox—apparently my eyebrows were the giveaway!

Although I've had short hair for my entire adult life, what has changed about my style is that it's becoming more flamboyant the older I get. It's liberating to embrace the quirkier parts of my personality and that's manifested itself in the colours I rinse through my hair and the way I team together my outfits in a more eccentric and vibrant way. It's exciting to push the hair envelope by dyeing my hair pink and shades of mauve. A couple of times I flaunted these shades on the television but that didn't go down well with my television bosses. However, I wasn't going to be dissuaded, so with my trademark stubbornness I just went a soft pink occasionally and acted 'surprised' that my hair had bizarrely ended up that colour! Somehow I think my boss saw through my amateur acting. But now that I've left my television role, I have relished introducing more colours of the rainbow to my long-suffering hair follicles. Mermaid-blue hair has been my latest flirtation.

Usually I'll speak to my husband a couple of times a day but recently, there was radio silence from me as I was at the salon while Pierre dyed my hair blue. I didn't tell Peter what I was doing as I knew he'd rant and rave about my colour choice. He already knew something was up, but nothing prepared him for my surprise! Peter walked slowly up our stairs after a long day at work and I was already hiding in bed, with a scarf over my head!

'Daddy, wait until you see what Mummy has done!' Giselle called out, as she heard her father on the stairs.

'What do you mean?' replied Peter, as he walked to our bedroom door to see me throw my flower-patterned scarf off with a flourish.

'Ta-dah!' I said.

Peter didn't say a word and just walked back down the stairs, furious. An hour later he returned wondering when he would get his blonde wife back.

'Please, Pussycat, I just want my golden retriever-coloured wife! Please . . . even pink. Pink would be better than this. It looks like you're ready to go to the nursing home!'

I reminded Peter that this blue hair would have gone perfectly with that mermaid dress I had worn all those years ago. Unfortunately, he wasn't ready to see the humour in that but for now he has his pink wife back. Well, that's for this month anyway.

CHICKEN AND PESTO SPAGHETTI

This twist on pesto pasta is courtesy of the super-talented Justine Schofield. This *MasterChef* alumni showed me how to make this easy meal that's in her recipe book *Simple Every Day*. It's an easy midweek dinner with protein so my husband can't say he needs more meat!

Ingredients
1 tbsp cooking oil
400 g chicken mince (first time I'd ever cooked chook mince—and as you know I love a mince recipe)
400 g spaghetti
1 jar of pesto sauce (Justine has a recipe for fresh pesto, but I love anything in a jar)
parmesan to serve

Method
Place large frying pan over high heat and add 1 tbsp of oil. Add the mince and cook. It's ready once the chicken has turned white and is cooked through (it takes about 5 minutes). Sprinkle some salt and pepper over the top.

Meanwhile, bring a large saucepan of water to the boil. Add the spaghetti and cook for around 8 minutes. Once you've drained the pasta, put it in the frying pan with the chicken mince and then stir the pesto sauce through.

Sprinkle parmesan over the top to serve.

Success rate

Three out of four family members enjoy this meal. Giselle will only eat pasta with bolognaise or tomato sauce at the moment. Also, she's not keen on anything green so that's another mark against the pesto sauce. But I know it can all change next week!

12

Cats

Time spent with cats is never wasted.

SIGMUND FREUD

I'm a crazy cat lady. No, I'm not a cat fancier, cat enthusiast or a cat lover. I've heard some cat fans shy away from the term 'crazy cat lady'. And I'm not sure why, perhaps they don't like the connotation of being a lady with hair rollers, who lives in a dressing gown, surrounded by her motley group of felines friends. Well, I often love to snuggle into my fleecy leopard-print dressing gown at home, my hair's way too short for rollers and I only have three cats but I'm happy to wear the label of being a crazy cat lady!

My house is full of all manner of cat paraphernalia: cushions, cups, figurines, doona covers, salt and pepper shakers, coasters, snow domes and prints. Many of my clothes have varying degrees of cat prints: dresses, T-shirts, unitards, coats, pyjamas, undies, socks, sneakers and stilettos. Not surprisingly, I also have a fine collection of earrings, rings, bracelets and necklaces all with a cat(s) featured somewhere in the design. Some of my more thoughtful friends often send me links about the latest cat-featured fashion.

What is it that I love about cats? They're elegant, stylish, wild, feral, independent, clean, aloof and, like my daughters, they don't always come when you call them. I've also found cats to be the ideal companions; they're uncompromising and won't suffer fools but they're also intuitive. Cats have a way of picking up on your mood and will either respond appropriately or not so appropriately. And it's in my adult years that I've formed special connections with cats who have turned out to be loyal, loving and kept me from being lonely.

#CRAPHOUSEWIFE

Quite simply, I've been mad about cats since I was a little girl. In an early black-and-white photo that I recently tore out of my mum's album, there's an image of me as a three-year-old. In this picture I'm already aligned with two of my great loves—dressing up and cats. On the top of my head I'm wearing an over-sized white cloche-style hat. My eyes are hard to spot under the brim but what you can clearly see is the tight headlock that I've managed to get around the neck of a giant, patient ginger cat. None of us can remember who owned the cat or where it had come from, but it was probably one of my first early encounters with cats. And from that moment on, it has been love at first sight.

My first 'proper' pet cat was black as night and named Pinkie. Dad had found her lurking around the carpark at the back of the offices where he worked. She was without a collar and took an instant liking to him, sometimes rubbing herself against his ankles. Clearly, this friendly cat was a stray and my father decided she would make the perfect addition to our family. He surprised us with this black cat one evening and while we screamed excitedly, the terrified slinky cat leapt directly out of the cardboard box and straight into the maiden hair ferns hanging from our ceiling.

Pinkie stayed in the hanging plant in our hallway for a long time, her yellow eyes flashing through the luminous green leaves. This became her favourite place to hide and she used to launch herself out of the ferns, digging her claws into the shoulders of unsuspecting visitors. She wasn't terribly friendly but I still loved that cat. Despite getting scratched, I persisted with Pinkie and although she wasn't keen on cuddles, I kept trying to pat her along with attempting to strap her into my dollies' pram. And

I remember being devastated when she got hit by a car just a few months after she joined our family.

A little later there was another stray, jet-black cat, who I named Vanessa, and who was only in our lives for a short time before she too disappeared on a busy road. She wasn't into the hanging baskets but her preferred perching place became the top of our small black-and-white television set. Vanessa would drop her long black tail over the front of the screen and start flicking it slowly, left and right, while we tried to watch our favourite show *Bewitched*. If any of us tried to move her to get a better view of what magic spells the witch Samantha was trying to sort out, Vanessa would lash out with a swift swipe of her paw. She also wasn't a very cuddly cat but I still loved her so.

Another pussycat made her home with us when we moved into another neighbourhood away from a main road. My sisters and I have conflicting recollections about where this tortoiseshell pussycat came from but I'm sticking with the version that we bought her during an outing with our dad from Paddy's Market at Haymarket in the city. Just like Pinkie, this cat came home in a second-hand cardboard box. My sisters and I decided to call our new cat Mog after the cat in the *Mog the Cat* picture books Mum had read to us when we were tiny girls. Our Mog had white whiskers like wings and plenty of patches of orange and white fur through her short, stubby coat.

Although she was a very plain-looking cat, I adored her, and unlike Pinkie and Vanessa, I had managed to get her to sleep under my doona with me most evenings.

Moggy kept us company through our parents' divorce, Mum's illness and my rocky teenage years culminating in my final year at school. Sadly, as I got more self-absorbed Mog got less of my attention and decided to spend most days yowling loudly from the rooftop of our apartment building. Once Mum had managed to coax her down, the attention-starved cat would waste no time in jumping back onto the top of our roof. One day I came home from school to discover Mog was missing but Mum explained that she had to take her to the vet for a 'terrible abscess' that had suddenly appeared! It's now part of our family folklore that Mum took Mog to the vet to be put down, but she still won't own up to her part in Mog's demise.

#CRAPHOUSEWIFE

Cats were missing from my life for a while after I left home for university and then spent some time overseas. Once I was ready to settle back down and had moved in with my plastic-surgeon boyfriend, I decided it was time to get another cat. Audrey caught my eye at the RSPCA shelter in western Sydney. She was another tortoiseshell cat with impossibly long white whiskers but her fur was fluffy and long and she had a magnificent tail that looked like a feather duster. This beautiful cat was my constant companion for the next ten years. She survived an 8-metre fall from my laundry window when the pair of us lived in a high-rise in Sydney's Bellevue Hill.

Soon after, Audrey moved with me when I proudly signed the mortgage papers on my first apartment in Sydney near Clovelly Beach. She wasn't initially keen on Peter and used to launch herself and her claws into his long feet and twitching toes that would stick out of the bottom of the doona on my double bed. This cat wasn't used to sharing the bed with anyone but me and she wasn't happy being cooped up in this tiny unit with no grass or dirt under her paws. However, once she and I moved out of that unit and Peter and I moved into a small house together ahead of our wedding, Audrey started to settle down. Perhaps because she could sense my happiness it meant that she could also relax a little. And it meant she gave up her middle-of-the-night stealth attacks on my soon-to-be-husband.

#CRAPHOUSEWIFE

Thankfully, Peter has always been a cat person, having also grown up with them, so he took to Audrey despite their prickly early introductions. He was also keen to get another cat now that we were starting our life together. Not that I needed much more evidence that Peter was the man for me, but when I heard him being 'interviewed' on the phone by a cat breeder, I realised how special he was.

'Hello, Tom, I'd love to have one of your British blue kittens,' said Peter.

He had become enamoured of this breed of cats after seeing one of them at a mutual friend's house.

I couldn't hear what the breeder was saying at the other end of the phone. All I could hear was my husband's loud, booming, cat-proud voice.

'Yes, I've always been a cat person. I have a very good relationship with Jessica's cat, Audrey. And I've always had cats in my life . . . If you agree to us having one of your kittens, I would like to call him Alfie, as that was the name of my very first cat!'

Once Peter had hung up the phone, his great big smile revealed he had passed 'the test' and we had been successful in getting another cat for our fledgling family. Alfie is now fifteen years old and although his steel-grey, fuzzy-felt fur is looking less sleek, he still brings us so much joy all these years later. He now uses his claws to drag himself up onto the couch or our bed since his legs aren't as springy, a contrast to when we first brought him home as a cheeky spritely kitten who would leap around Audrey—the elegant older lady of the house.

Way before the sun woke up, Auds used to get up with me when my alarm went off at 3.20 a.m. for the *Today* show. She would wait outside the shower recess while I tried to wash the exhaustion and sleep from my body. Later, when I was going through IVF, and then pregnant with Allegra, she would curl herself up against my cramping and growing belly, keeping me company through those tentative days of hoping my baby would hold on and keep growing healthily inside of me. That loyal cat also stayed by my side while I raged against the dead of night during my postnatal depression. Again, she curled up against my stomach while I was pregnant with Giselle, purring and raising her soft, white chin for a gentle pat.

Although Audrey kept a wary distance from the girls who were always trying to grab her fat, fluffy tail or elegant whiskers with their sticky fingers, she would still follow me, wrapping and weaving herself between my legs. My daughters had inherited their parents' love of cats and were always trying to drag either Audrey or Alfie onto their beds each night. Life was good; we were happy to be a two-cat family for a couple of years. However, I was heartsick when we had to say goodbye to Audrey. She was full of disease and the vet recommended that it was best for her to go 'to sleep'. Cradling her like a child while I watched her peacefully slip away, I thanked this white-pawed pussycat for keeping me company through some of the loneliest and darkest times of my life. In my top drawer I still have her box of ashes and worn, fraying pink collar. Perhaps it might be time to scatter them under our giant ghost gum in the corner of our backyard.

It took a while to fill the hole that Audrey had left in our lives. I wasn't ready to fill that empty space on the bed or outside of the shower. Eventually, it meant the girls found their own cat, a brown Persian, which was being kept at the local vet because its owner was too frail to look after her anymore. We walked past the vet's window and this old brown cat stared longingly out of her cage at the three of us.

'Mumma, please, can we have her?' asked Allegra.

'Pwease . . .' repeated Giselle.

'She has such sad eyes, Mumma. Please, please can we take her home?'

Of course, I quickly relented and we sent Peter a picture of the newest addition to our family.

Coincidentally, the girls wanted to name their cat Vanessa, unaware that I'd had my own Vanessa at a similar age. For a time, this quiet, shy cat with an endearing flat face split her time between hiding under their beds or being dressed up and pushed around in my daughters' dollies' pram. I would laughingly point out to them that that was exactly what I'd done to my cat. Unfortunately, Vanessa was only with us for a short time as her ongoing health problems meant she joined Pinkie, Vanessa (the first one), Mog and Audrey on the giant, velvet couch they could forever scratch, in the sky.

#CRAPHOUSEWIFE

Since both of the girls were heartbroken after Vanessa's death, I gave them the task of finding a new cat for our family when they were ready. Allegra had become especially taken with ragdoll cats, not only because of their bright-blue eyes but because of their gentle, laid-back personalities. We found the perfect kitten at a home that was a few hours' drive away from Sydney.

Mum and my youngest sister Claudia decided to join the girls and me for our cat road trip. The four of them spent the return journey arguing over who could have our new kitten, still in her cage, on their lap. Allegra decided to name her cat Daisy and the name matches her sweet, easy personality. Daisy now spends her days either in dress-ups, in prams, wearing hats or sleeping curled up under an old rocking horse that I can't bear to throw out.

The newest addition to our cat family is Violet; she's a British blue like Alfie and although I'm biased I think she's the prettiest cat in the entire world with her mauve-and-white fur and the longest white whiskers. We had been a two-cat family for a long time but I had managed to convince my husband of the 'benefits' of a third cat. My argument was that Giselle has been especially close to Alfie, and she couldn't comprehend the idea that he would die one day. I thought that if we got her a cat of her own, it might make it easier to deal with Alfie's ageing. Thankfully, at fifteen years of age, Alfie is for now still going strong and we also have this cheeky little cat that tears around the house. She keeps the whole family on its toes with her hyperactive antics and meerkat manoeuvres.

So, now we have three and I would still love to get another cat. Allegra is particularly keen to have 'her own' cat for her next birthday. Recently, when we were at the pet shop, she was in floods of tears to leave the kittens behind. However, I fear that three cats might be our limit because even though I have married a cat man I know that if I tried to sneak another cat into our house I might be stretching his patience, which is already often stretched tautly by the three crazy cat ladies in his life!

HAMBURGERS

Who doesn't like a burger? This easy meal has become a weekly addition to our menu, as it's simple to cater to individual (fussy) tastes with the addition/removal of cheese, tomato, avocado and lettuce.

Ingredients

4 hamburger patties (supermarket bought)

sliced cheese (depending on whether someone wants cheese)

4 hamburger buns (we use the sweeter 'Sonoma bakery hamburger buns' but there are so many varieties to choose from at the supermarket)

3 truss tomatoes

1 avocado

1 small cos lettuce (chopped)

tomato sauce

Method

Preheat oven to 180 degrees Celsius. Lightly brown each side of the hamburger patties in a frypan. A revelation for me has been putting these browned patties into the oven to finish off the cooking process! Previously my meat patties would be raw in the middle and burnt on the outside, until I learnt this sensational tip from some other crap housewives on Instagram. Usually the patties will take about 15–20 minutes to cook.

Once they're cooked, I put cheese on top of the patties for those who want cheese, and keep them in the oven for another couple of minutes to melt.

Finally, assemble your burger with whatever fillings take your fancy.

Success rate

Four out of four family members love this meal. It's a winner!

Epilogue

With freedom, books, flowers, and the moon,
who could not be happy?

OSCAR WILDE

As I jump into the cool, clean water, the rush of bubbles tickles my nose as my feet push up off the bottom of the pool. I start laughing just as my daughters and I break the surface of the water at the same time.

'Mummy, you were meant to hold our hands the whole time,' said Allegra.

'Sweetness, I didn't mean to let go,' I replied.

'Come on, let's do it again, but this time, Mumma, you can't let go,' said Giselle.

'Alright, I promise,' I said, as the three of us clambered out of the water and walked back to the deep end.

It has been a year since my sea change and we've returned as a family to that same turquoise-tiled pool in Thailand where I made that choice to change the direction of my life. And as I let the hot, humid heat dry my skin, I have no regrets about stepping back from my career and stepping up for my family.

It has taken a while for my mind to adjust to the slower, calmer pace of life. Initially it was strange to have a diary no longer crammed with commitments. But I have learnt to appreciate those longer gaps between places I needed to go and people who I needed to see. Gradually I realised the freedom that came from choosing to spend time with people that mattered most to me, rather than letting them down because of the demands of a busy, crazed life. And also the relief of letting go of the people who weren't good for my spirit and self-worth.

This year I have spent more time with my girls, my husband, my family and friends. And the best part of that, according to my youngest daughter Giselle, is that I'm around to take her to school each day. Allegra says she loves being able to spend more time with me and that 'I'm so less stressed'. And Peter says, despite the chaos I've brought to his morning routine, my change has been a game changer for our family.

What hasn't changed is the daily mess that makes up our lives. I'm not a better cook, housekeeper or organiser.

But in my heart, I know I'm a happier person because my life is calmer and less fraught. I'm still seeking out adventures but I'm going for opportunities that work best for me and my family and where we're at in our lives.

My leap into the deep blue has been worth it. And I know there will be plenty more of these leaps of faith for me. Bring on the next chapter for this crap housewife . . .

Acknowledgements

Thank you to my publisher Annette Barlow and her fine team at Allen & Unwin. Annette has been coaxing me to get the words onto the page for over twenty years and I wouldn't trust my stories or heart with anyone else. Fiona Inglis, my literary agent who has looked after my mother and me since we wrote our first book together and she has kept our words in print! My dream team of David Wilson and Andrew Gaul from Watercooler Talent. I love these wonderful men, who are family to me and have kept believing in me and my quirky, wondrous ways when no one else would.

Thank you to Justine Schofield, Adam Liaw, 4 Ingredients, Ash Pollard and Paula Joye for letting me reproduce their recipes and for revolutionising my weekly meals.

To Woffy, my darling friend, who first encouraged me to write this diary. Thank you Pip, my zone one pal, who told me that Agatha Christie wrote her books in a tent on an archaeological dig in Mesopotamia, so I could write my book anywhere and I needed to get cracking on it! My Mesopotamia became the local library, a haven for writers and students everywhere. Thank you to the librarians, even if I was a little noisy at times for the other occupants.

Finally, endless love and thanks to my Petee. I couldn't do any of this, or life, without YOU.